THE BOOK OF
JOSEPH

REVELATIONS OF THE LIFE, DEATH, AND GLORIFICATION OF THE VIRGIN FATHER OF CHRIST

José A. Rodrigues

Imprimatur:
✠ Ramón C. Argüelles, STL
Archbishop-Emeritus of Lipa
Date: 12.09.2019

Published by Ad Te Beate Ioseph,
www.BookOfJoseph2017.wixsite.com/SaintJoseph
Printed in Canada by First Choice Books, www.FirstChoiceBooks.ca

Bible Abbreviations:
DRV – Douay-Rheims Version
ESV – English Standard Version
NAB – New American Bible
NASB – New American Standard Bible
NIV – New International Version
NRSV – New Revised Standard Version
NRSVCE – New Revised Standard Version Catholic Edition
RSV – Revised Standard Version
RSVCE – Revised Standard Version Catholic Edition
WBT – Webster Bible Translation

PART ONE: YOUNG ST. JOSEPH

PART TWO: THE VIRGIN FATHER

PART THREE: THE COMMUNION OF SAINTS

PART SIX: POPES, SAINTS, & FEAST DAYS

PART SEVEN: PRAYER & SCRIPTURE

This humble book is dedicated to Fr. Paul Tinguely for his spiritual and temporal assistance, fatherly friendship, and for putting up with me over the years. This good priest, though he would strongly deny it, is a saint in my eyes.

Special thanks to Benjamin Adams, Jonathan to my David (1 Samuel 18:1-4).

HIS HOLINESS POPE FRANCIS
Angelus 22 December 2013

Joseph was a man who always listened to the voice of God, he was deeply sensitive to His secret will, he was a man attentive to the messages that came to him from the depths of his heart and from on High. He did not persist in following his own plan for his life, he did not allow bitterness to poison his soul; rather, he was ready to make himself available to God's plan. And thus, he was a good man. He did not hate. Yet how many times does hatred, or even dislike and bitterness poison our souls? This is harmful, never allow it: he is an example of this. Joseph thereby became even freer and greater. By accepting himself according to God's design, Joseph fully finds himself, beyond himself. His freedom to renounce even what is his, the possession of his very life, and his full interior availability to the will of God challenges us and shows us the way (Francis, 2013).

FOREWORD

The Book of Joseph is about St. Joseph, the Spouse of our Blessed Mother Mary and the Virgin Father of Jesus. As a priest, in reading José's book, I am amazed at the points that he makes about the royalty, the chastity, the youthfulness, and of the importance of this intercessor in the life of the Church. There are good points of reflection which challenge the 'old' ideas that we may have of St. Joseph, such as him being a widower, of being an old man and of having his own children. These notions are not accepted in this book! It is refreshing to hear enunciated in this book the tradition of the Church about this saint and to bring out, as a result, a more vibrant image of who Joseph really was and still is.

Many references are made by the privileged insights of three women seers from their writings on the life of the Holy Family. Two of them are not yet Saints of the Church, one being honoured as Venerable and the other as Blessed. Popes, Church Fathers, and known Saints are quoted throughout the book which gives credibility to the text.

And finally, the book includes a series of prayers, recognized and accepted by the Church, which become an easy to find source of needed prayer when we especially hear the advice of the Popes and Saints: "Go to Joseph".

Father Paul Tinguely, p.p.

INTRODUCTION

St. Joseph is the reflection of God the Father, Guardian of God the Son, Friend of God the Holy Spirit, and Spouse of the Immaculate Handmaiden. In his youth, he prayed for the coming of the promised Messiah. In his adult life, not only were his prayers answered, but he *loved* and *upheld* the Messiah, Jesus Christ. And now, in the Court of Heaven, St. Joseph intercedes for the Church before the throne of Christ.

Although he has the status of *protodulia* (venerated above all saints, excepting the Virgin Mary), St. Joseph is easily written off by people with the same excuse "we know very little about him, the Bible does not record a single spoken word by him", when in truth we *do* know a lot about him - we just need to search for him.

In the journey to find St. Joseph, one comes to discover that there is in fact *a lot* to learn about him in the words of the Saints, Mystics and Popes of the Church. The problem is that a lot of these wordy, technical writings were unapproachable for many of the faithful, and have since gone unnoticed through the centuries.

Wanting to share St. Joseph with everyone but knowing that in this day and age many people have little time to read lengthy, fine print, scholarly volumes of books, the author decided to do the research and present the findings under one cover. After the information was gathered from various sources, the life of St. Joseph was pieced together as a single narrative. It was a difficult task to select what to include and what to leave out, but, in the end, the essentials have been provided.

The words of Church-approved Mystics, Saints, Blessed, Venerable, and Popes, not only present the story of St. Joseph but they also give insight into the beliefs of these important figures in Church history.

Works of art have been included to help the reader reflect not only on some of the important events in Joseph's life, but also showcase different *styles* of art from around the world.

With the hope that people will be drawn into forming a personal devotion to him, a section on prayers to St. Joseph has been included. These include the Holy Cloak, Chaplet, and other prayers.

Though the author is no theologian, professor, lecturer, or any other type of authority on this matter, there was a need to write this book and to share it with the hopes that people might gain something good from it, whether it be a better understanding of St. Joseph, a prayer they have never prayed, or even an image they have never seen. Therefore, this humble book is presented to the reader in the hopes that they will read this with an open heart and an open mind.

May God bless you and St. Joseph smile upon you!

José A. Rodrigues

PART ONE: YOUNG ST. JOSEPH

I will pour out my spirit upon thy seed, and my blessing upon thy stock (Isaiah 44:3 DRV).

CHAPTER 1: THE INFANT PRINCE

This chapter speaks of the venerable parents of St. Joseph, the miraculous circumstances of his conception and birth, his circumcision and presentation, and his early gift of reason.

ST. JOSEPH'S FATHER

By the time of the birth of Christ, Judea had been lost to the Romans and the descendants of King David had lost their royal birthright and their place in line for the throne. Herod the Great, who was appointed king of the Jews by the Roman senate, had usurped the throne. Joseph of Nazareth, the earthly father of Jesus (though not according to the flesh), was a part of this Davidic lineage and remained the rightful heir of the kings of Judea. The Bible traces his genealogy in the Gospel of St. Matthew, naming his father to be Jacob, a descendant of David:

> ... Abraham begot Isaac, Isaac begot Jacob ... Jesse begot David the king. And David the king begot Solomon ... Matthan begot Jacob. And Jacob begot Joseph, the husband of Mary, of whom was born Jesus, who is called Christ (Matthew 1:1-16 DRV).

Then how does one explain the genealogy given in the Gospel of St. Luke? In this account Joseph is still a descendent of King David, but his father is not Jacob but rather Heli:

> And Jesus himself was beginning about the age of thirty years; being (as it was supposed) the son of Joseph, the son of Heli, the son of Matthat, the son of Levi ... Nathan the son of David ... (Luke 3:23, 31 DRV).

Heli (also known as Joachim) was the father of the Blessed Virgin Mary, St. Joseph's bride. According to the Law, upon marrying the Virgin Mary, Joseph's "legal father" or "father-in-law" became Heli. In St. Matthew's account, the word "begot" is used when descending the family tree, this refers to biological fathers or at guardians thought of as fathers. In St. Luke's account, the words "son of" are used instead of "begot." This may refer to "son in the eyes of the law."

However, many of the names in St. Luke's account are also biological fathers, so this may cause confusion. One must now look to other divinely inspired sources for confirmation that Jacob was indeed St. Joseph's biological father. Per the visions of the German Mystic Blessed Anne Catherine Emmerich (1774-1824), St. Joseph's father was indeed Jacob, as confirmed by other mystics as well as was prefigured in the Old Testament:

> Joseph's grandfather Matthan had descended from David through Solomon. He had two sons, Joses and Jacob. Jacob was Joseph's father (A. Emmerich, 1953, pg. 17).

ST. JOSEPH'S MOTHER AND SIBLINGS

The father of St. Joseph was Jacob; however, the Bible is silent on the matter of who his mother was. Since the Joseph of the Old Testament appears to prefigure that of the New, and both testaments name Jacob as the name of both fathers, one may piously believe that Rachel is the name of both mothers.

For the identity of Joseph's mother one may choose to look to the *Nihil Obstat* and *Imprimatur* granted writings of the Servant of God, mystic Mother Cecilia Baij (1694-1766) who, as Abbess of the Benedictine Convent of St. Peter in Montefiascone, Italy, received revelations from Our Lord Jesus in the mid-18th century:

St. Joseph's father's name was Jacob and his mother's name was Rachel. Both distinguished themselves by leading very holy lives; they had in common nobility of birth (both were of the family of David) (C. Baij, 1997, pg.1).

As to the question of Joseph having siblings, Blessed Anne Catherine Emmerich reveals that he had five brothers. Most other mystics, however, claim that St. Joseph was an only child. These "brothers" mentioned by Emmerich were possibly cousins who at times lived with Joseph's family or perhaps Joseph lived with them for a time. Per Church tradition, and as chronicled by St. Hegesippus (110-180), Cleophas, also referred to as Alpheus, was a relative to St. Joseph who was sometimes referred to as his brother. He was wed to the Virgin Mary's cousin, who was also named Mary. He is mentioned in the Gospel of St. John (19:25) and St. Luke (24:18).

THE CONCEPTION & SANCTIFICATION OF JOSEPH

Before I formed thee in the bowels of thy mother, I knew thee: and before thou camest forth out of the womb, I sanctified thee (Jeremiah 1:5 DRV).

Through the Servant of God, Mother Cecilia Baij, whose writings have been acclaimed for centuries, the circumstances of St. Joseph's conception and birth are known. These events mirror those of the prophet Jeremiah (Jeremiah 1:5) and St. John the Baptist (Luke 1:5-19, 41-44) who were sanctified in the womb, and were blessings to their families. They were freed from the stain of original sin by the grace of God *after* their conception, not to be confused with the *Immaculate* conception of the Blessed Virgin Mary.

Joseph's father, Jacob, was born in Nazareth whereas his mother, Rachel, was born in Bethlehem. Both were descendants of King David and lived together in Nazareth, leading very holy lives. Though they were full of virtue, God deigned to leave them childless for a time, as sorrowful as it was for them, in order that ...

... Joseph be a child obtained through prayerful entreaty. To this purpose, his parents generously bestowed alms upon the poor and for the Temple in Jerusalem. They also made many pilgrimages to beg God for the desired offspring (C. Baij, 1997, pg. 1).

It was not long before God rewarded Jacob and Rachel with the conception of their much prayed for son, with signs and angelic messages announcing that the child was especially chosen and beloved by God. Mother Cecelia Baij continues:

It was on one occasion while in the Temple, that Joseph's mother experienced an inner conviction that God had heard her prayer ... and indeed she conceived St. Joseph.

At this time, three unusually bright stars, surpassing one another in beauty and splendor, could be seen directly above their home ... An angel came to them and revealed certain mysterious and secret facts concerning this child. And the angel said to them:

"This child resting beneath his mother's heart will have the happy privilege of seeing the promised Messiah and associating with Him. You are to rear him with special foresight and diligence, training and instructing him in the Sacred Scriptures. You shall call his name 'Joseph' and he will be great in the sight of God (C. Baij, 1997, pg. 2)!"

In the seventeenth century, the Spanish mystic Maria de Agreda (1602-1665) was also given heavenly insights into the life of St. Joseph. Her writings have been beloved throughout the centuries by Popes and theologians, and she has since been declared Venerable by the Church and is now on the path to beatification. She too was shown that St. Joseph's conception was miraculous:

> Joseph was to be a miracle of holiness. This marvelous holiness commenced with the formation of his body in the womb of his mother. In this the providence of God Himself intervened, regulating the composition of his body with extreme nicety of proportion and securing for him that evenly tempered disposition which made his body a blessed fit for the abode of an exquisite soul and well-balanced mind (Wisdom 8:19.)

> He was sanctified in the womb of his mother seven months after his conception, and the leaven of sin was destroyed in him for the whole course of life (M. Agreda, 1912, p. 163).

St. Alphonsus de Liguori also believed that, for good reason, St. Joseph was sanctified in his mother's womb:

> When God, destines anyone for a particular office, He gives him the graces that fit him for it. Among those granted, Joseph had three which were special to him. Firstly, that he was sanctified in his mother's womb, as were Jeremias and St. John the Baptist. Secondly, that he was at the same time confirmed in grace. And thirdly, that he was always exempt from

the inclinations of concupiscence (A. Liguori, 1962, pg. 5).

THE BIRTH OF JOSEPH

During this time of holy expectation, Jacob and Rachel immersed themselves in prayer, giving to the poor, and observed periods of fasting – all in thanksgiving to God for the coming of their promised son. When the day for the little prince to be born into the world finally arrived, Mother Cecelia Baij reveals:

> Joseph's mother gave birth to him with ease. The tiny babe had a most angelic, venerable, and serene expression ... and the mere sight of him was an occasion of spiritual stimulation for everyone. The news of the birth of this child, and the unusual circumstances connected with it, spread throughout Nazareth. This child was said to be a veritable "angel of paradise," and all were elated (C. Baij, 1997, pg. 3).

The three stars again appeared over the house as Joseph was being born and were observed with astonishment. Joseph, upon opening his little eyes, directed them heavenwards, and for a while kept them fixed upon these stars, the signs God had given to announce his birth.

Joseph was in the grace and friendship of God, having been previously freed of the stain of original sin. ... His soul's growth was derived from the graces he obtained from the divine bounty and generosity. God fashioned him according to His own heart and spirit, in order to eventually make him a worthy bridegroom for the Mother of the Divine Word (C. Baij, 1997, pg. 4, 5).

THE CIRCUMCISION AND PRESENTATION OF JOSEPH

Concerning the little prince, the Scriptures do not give any account of his childhood. As with the story of his conception and birth, one must look to the divinely inspired writings of Mother Cecelia Baij for details of Joseph's circumcision, his early gift of reason, and his presentation in the Temple.

> On the octave day of his birth, the parents had Joseph circumcised ... and he was given the name of "Joseph" (which means: May the Lord Give Increase). Though crying at first, the infant soon became quiet for among the many gifts which God had now bestowed upon him was the use of reason. And due to his sanctification in the womb, being freed of the stain of original sin, Joseph was already in the friendship of God (C. Baij, 1997, pg. 5).

> Forty days after the birth of Joseph his parents brought him to the Jerusalem Temple to present him ... As the priest took Joseph into his arms, and presented and offered him to God, he experienced an extraordinary sensation of joy and consolation of spirit.

> The priest ... perceived how pleasing this child was in the eyes of God. During the entire ritual Joseph's eyes were open and directed towards Heaven, being completely taken up and absorbed in God. ... The priest revealed them that this child was pleasing to God, and was destined for great things ... After

21

hearing this, the parents gave thanks to God, ... their hearts profoundly touched and filled with joy. They carried Joseph home as a treasure, as a divinely conferred gift (C. Baij, 1997, pg. 6, 7).

CHAPTER 2: THE CHILD JOSEPH

This chapter speaks of the education of the child Joseph, his piety, his angel companions, and the attacks of the devil.

THE EDUCATION AND PIETY OF THE CHILD JOSEPH

As the child Joseph grew, he matured quickly in intelligence, in awareness of God, and in angelic virtues. As revealed by Venerable Maria de Agreda, Mother Cecelia Baij and Blessed Anne Catherine Emmerich, this was the result of the work God had done in sanctifying him and blessing him with early use of reason, and the teaching of Scripture by his father Jacob.

> The Lord hastened the use of Joseph's reason, endowing it with infused science and augmenting his soul with new graces and virtues. The child began to know God as the cause and Author of all things. He eagerly listened and understood profoundly all that was taught him in regard to God and His works. He was of a kind disposition, loving, and affable, sincere, showing inclinations not only holy but angelic, growing in virtue and perfection (M. Agreda, 1912, p. 164).

> Joseph was privileged to talk very early, his first words being "My God!" ... When Joseph's parents saw how intelligent he already was, they began instructing him in reading. This the father took upon himself as he was well versed in the Law. Joseph began to learn to read, and he managed remarkably well. He soon advanced to the reading of the Sacred Scriptures, and especially the Davidic Psalms, all of which his father explained to him. This provided Joseph with much joy. Joseph had a great veneration

for the patriarchs, Abraham, Isaac and Jacob, as well as for the prophet David. He often asked his father to tell him the stories of their lives. Joseph had the desire to imitate them when he saw how they were loved and specially privileged by God (C. Baij, 1997, pg. 12, 16).

When he heard his father relate how Abraham had always lived in the presence of God, Joseph was determined to imitate him. And truly, Joseph had already acquired by the age of seven, a true appreciation of all the virtues that the patriarchs had practiced (C. Baij, 1997, pg. 17).

At this premature age, he already practiced the highest kinds of prayer and contemplation and eagerly engaged in the exercise of the virtues proper to his youth; so that, at the time when others come to the use of reason, at the age of seven years or more, saint Joseph was already a perfect man in the use of it and in holiness (M. Agreda, 1912, p. 164).

Joseph, whom I saw in this vision at about the age of eight, was very gifted and was a very good scholar. He was simple, quiet, devout, and unpretentious. ... His inclinations were towards working at some quiet handicraft, and prayer. I often saw him kneeling with his face to the wall, praying with outstretched arms (A. Emmerich, 1953, pg. 76).

JOSEPH'S ANGEL COMPANIONS AND THE DEVIL'S ATTACKS

As the child Joseph continued to grow the devil took notice of him. He was aware that Joseph was unlike other children. This child possessed the reasoning and virtues of a grown man, lived piously, and communed with angels. The devil knew that Joseph would one day associate with the Messiah when He came but did not know in what capacity. The devil was confused; he did not fully know what this boy's role was in God's redemptive plan, but he made war on him regardless, as Mother Cecelia Baij acknowledges:

> The devil, that hellish fiend, was aware of the light that abided in Joseph and he feared that this child would arouse others to take up the struggle against him. He attempted several times to take the child's life, but his plans always went awry, for Joseph was protected by the almighty arm of God. Joseph was guarded by two angels ... and the angel who had been assigned to speak to him in his dreams continually advised him on what to do to overcome the infernal demon ... Joseph never failed to carry out the admonitions of the angel   (C. Baij, 1997, 10, 11).

Seeing the difficulty posed by the child's protective angels, the devil then decided to go after those close to Joseph, namely his parents and the domestic servants. He tried to instill in them hostility and confusion with the desired outcome of mistreatment and abuse of little Joseph. Mother Cecelia Baij continues:

> The devil devised another ruse, whereby, he endeavored to instigate strife and confusion between Joseph's parents. This too failed. ... Satan then attempted an attack upon the domestics of the

household, but even this miscarried, for Joseph prayed for them all and God heard his petitions (C. Baij, 1997, pg. 11).

The angel who had been assigned to speak to Joseph in his dreams continually advised him in how to overcome the demon. He would inform Joseph as soon as he saw that the devil was preparing to launch another attack against the household, and Joseph never failed to carry out the admonitions of the angel.

> The devil often endeavored to stir up the domestics to mistreat Joseph, for the purpose of seeing him fail in the virtue of patience during affliction. But in this the demon never succeeded (C. Baij, 1997, pg. 16).

The devil, being increasingly angry and frustrated, then instilled in some of the townspeople a great hatred for Joseph, inciting them to abuse him in various ways. It is revealed that among them, the devil chose to act through, as Mother Cecelia writes, "undisciplined youths" and "a woman who led an evil life":

> Satan continued in his harassment of Joseph by stirring up against him a number of people who were leading bad lives; he implanted in them a great hatred for this holy soul ... Undisciplined youths agreed to bombard him with invective whenever they would meet him ... they would scoff and jeer at him. The saintly Joseph would merely bow his head ... and beg God that his enemies would be enlightened and realize their error. When the youths observed this, they labeled him a blockhead, a coward, and a frightened rabbit. Joseph calmly continued on his way. The youths followed him, hurling at him their offensive language (C. Baij, 1997, pg. 26).

The devil made use of a woman who, because of her evil life, hated the very sight of the little Saint. He incited her to go often to Joseph's mother in order to harass her and to report falsehoods against her son. ... Although he knew who was causing all the trouble, Joseph's heart bore no hostility (C. Baij, 1997, pg. 27).

The harassment endured by Joseph is also revealed in the writings of Blessed Anne Catherine Emmerich, and further by Mother Cecelia Baij, who were shown visions of these events:

I often saw young Joseph under the colonnade in the outer court kneeling with his face to the wall, praying ... and I saw the boys creep up and kick him. I once saw him kneeling like this, when one of them hit him on the back, and as he did not seem to notice it, he repeated his attack with such violence that poor Joseph fell forward onto the hard, stone floor. From this I realized that he was not in a waking condition but had been in an ecstasy of prayer. When he came to himself, he did not lose his temper or take revenge, but found a hidden corner where he continued his prayer (A. Emmerich, 1953, pg. 76).

The sight of this virtuous child put the devil into a frightful rage. He became violent, and undertook one day, to cast Joseph down headlong over a flight of stairs ... Joseph called to God for help and the Most High prevented him from being harmed ... the devil was now forced to withdraw (C. Baij, 1997, pg. 17).

The purposes of these attacks by the devil were not just meant to produce some physical harm to Joseph, but to destroy or at least diminish his spirituality, his sanctity, by causing him to despair and to retaliate hatred with hatred. But this did not happen. Through all this, the child Joseph prayed for those who mistreated him, with the maturity of a grown man but with the innocence of a child. Mother Cecelia Baij and Pope Francis reflect on the peace of St. Joseph, even in difficult times:

> Joseph was so submerged in the thought of God's love, and so joyful over the realization of God's presence in his soul, that nothing could disturb the peace within his heart (C. Baij, 1997, pg. 17).

> St. Joseph did not allow bitterness to poison his soul; rather, he was ready to make himself available to God's plan. He did not hate. Yet how many times does hatred, or even dislike and bitterness poison our souls! And this is harmful. Never allow it: Joseph is an example of this (Francis, 2013).

CHAPTER 3: THE ADOLESCENCE AND EARLY MANHOOD

This chapter speaks of the sinless adolescence of Joseph, the death of his parents, his work as a carpenter, and his vow of virginity.

Time passed since the harassments of the devil, and the young Joseph continued to live a sinless life as he grew in body, wisdom, and in the constant friendship of God. He also began learning the skills of basic carpentry. Blessed Anne Catherine Emmerich and Servant of God Mother Cecelia Baij reveal this time in Joseph's life:

> When Joseph was about twelve years old, I often saw him visiting the caves where he would pray alone. He also enjoyed making all kinds of little things out of wood; for there was an old carpenter who had a workshop with whom Joseph spent much of his time. He helped him with his work and so little by little learnt his craft (A. Emmerich, 1953, pg. 77).

> As he grew older Joseph made great strides in the practice of virtue, in the love for God, and in the study of the Scriptures, especially the Davidic Psalms. His life developed along these lines for fifteen years without causing in God any displeasure, committing neither mortal sin, nor any deliberate venial sin: and he made every effort to avoid even the very shadow of sin (C. Baij, 1997, pg. 33, 34).

THE DEATH OF JOSEPH'S PARENTS

For any accounting of the deaths of Joseph's parents the only source of information comes from the revelations of Mother

Cecilia Baij, as no other venerable or saint has appeared to come forward with such details.

It has been revealed that St. Joseph was eighteen years of age when his parents died. His mother was first to die due to illness. It was Joseph, who would one day become the Patron of a Happy Death, who ministered to her in her last days. In her final moments, she experienced great happiness and consolation in the presence of her holy son:

> Joseph was eighteen years of age when, according to God's will, his parents departed from this earthly life. He rendered to his mother a most commendable assistance and service, strengthening and comforting her in her pain, constantly begging God to give her patience in her agonizing illness (C. Baij, 1997, pg. 39).

The holy youth spent many a night watching, assisting, and praying at his mother's bedside. Just as he had shown his gratitude for her goodness to him, so now in these last moments of her life, his behavior was exemplary. He did not wish to leave her, and never tired of serving and comforting her with his truly childlike, yet holy love.

> Joseph remained with her until she expired. He was a great help not only to her, but also to his father, who was sorely grieved over the loss of so virtuous a companion in life (C. Baij, 1997, pg. 40).

St. Joseph, suffering the loss of his mother, had little time to grieve, as it was soon after her departure that his father had become ill. He would continue in his role as devoted son to his father, just as he had done for his mother, ministering to him in his final moments:

It was not long afterwards that Joseph's father became deathly sick. Joseph himself had been weakened considerably during the period of his mother's painful illness, to which was now added his father's serious affliction. … Joseph tended and served his father affectionately, both day and night, and encouraged him in the patient endurance of his sufferings and anxieties. As his father's last hours arrived, Joseph attended him lovingly, encouraging … and consoling him with his own conviction that he would soon enter the domain of peace and joy. Thus, fully resigned and with a firm hope of obtaining eternal life, Joseph's father finally expired. Once his father had breathed his last, Joseph withdrew and allowed his grief-stricken nature to find relief in tears. Indeed, he had every reason to be sorrowful, considering what a generous, loving and solicitous father he had lost (C. Baij, 1997, pg. 41).

After the departure of his father, the image of eighteen-year-old Joseph falling under the weight of his tears is shown, not only allowing himself to grieve the loss of his parents whom he loved so dearly, but also commending himself, with filial trust, to the care of the Heavenly Father. Mother Cecelia Baij continues:

Joseph fell upon his knees, and in tears, besought the Divine Majesty for aid with these words: "Oh God! … Look down upon me, deprived of both father and mother. You have graciously placed them beyond reach of the cares of this mortal life, and I now beg You, that in Your goodness You take me entirely under Your protection. I give and surrender myself entirely to You. … Since I am no longer subject to anyone but You, my God, give me the needed grace, so that I too may be able to say with the royal prophet: 'My father and mother have left me, but the Lord has taken me up' (Psalm 27:10). Do with me as it pleases You. May Your holy will be accomplished in me (C. Baij, 1997, pg. 44)."

JOSEPH APPRENTICES AS A CARPENTER AND LATER MOVES TO TIBERIAS WHERE HE IS VISITED BY ONE OF HIS ANGELS

It has been revealed by Blessed Anne Catherine Emmerich that, at around the age of nineteen, St. Joseph moved to a place called Lebona, which was on the south side of Mount Gerizim. It was here that he apprenticed under a carpenter. After this, at the age of thirty-three, he moved to Tiberias, on the West shore of the Sea of Galilee, where he continued working as a carpenter:

> Joseph might have been eighteen to twenty years old at that time. I saw him working with a carpenter at Lebona. This was the place where he first learnt his craft. Joseph was very devout, good, and not at all complicated, everybody loved him. I saw him helping his master very humbly. Later still I saw him working in Tiberius for a master-carpenter. He was thirty-three years old at that time. Joseph was very devout and prayed fervently for the coming of the Messiah.

It was while he was working here that his angel appeared to him with a cryptic message:

> "As once the patriarch Joseph had, by God's will, been made overseer of all the corn of Egypt, so you, the new Joseph, should now be entrusted with the

care of the granary of salvation." St. Joseph in his humility did not understand this, and gave himself up to continual prayer, until he received the call to betake himself to Jerusalem (A. Emmerich, 1953, pg. 77, 78).

JOSEPH VOWS HIS VIRGINITY TO GOD

The angel did not take long in returning to Joseph to give the command that he was to move to Jerusalem where he would begin to enter the mystery of which he was told very little. While at Jerusalem, Joseph is told by the angel of the Virgin Mary and is inspired to make his own vow of virginity to God. Mother Cecelia Baij reveals:

> The angel appeared to Joseph and advised him to go to Jerusalem ... where at the Temple there was a maiden who was most dear to God, and for whom God had a special love. This Temple virgin was Mary, the daughter of Joachim and Anna. ... He was told that Mary had dedicated herself entirely to God, and had vowed to Him her virginity, with which God was pleased. Joseph felt the desire to do the same, and he dedicated his virginity to God by means of a vow. Since this was a most unusual thing for a man to do, the Saint was undecided if he could do so, and if it would be pleasing to God. ... As he made his promise of perpetual virginity to God, Joseph's heart was filled with an inexpressible joy. God permitted him to feel this so that he might be assured of how pleasing this vow was to Him. He was then raised to a delightful ecstasy in which God manifested to him

the merit of the virtue of chastity (C. Baij, 1997, pg. 53, 54).

For thou hast done manfully, and thy heart has been strengthened, because thou hast loved chastity (Judith 15:11 DRV).

CHAPTER 4: A SON OF DAVID IS SUMMONED

This chapter speaks of the summoning of the sons of David to the Temple to find a suitable husband for the Virgin Mary and discusses the royalty of St. Joseph, his stolen birthright, and his feeling of unworthiness.

As Joseph worked and lived in Jerusalem, a decree went out from the Temple to all the unmarried male descendants of King David: All sons of the royal House of David were to report to the Jerusalem Temple in order that a suitable husband for the Temple Virgin, Mary, daughter of Heli (Joachim), be chosen from among them. Joseph, being a son of David, was required to report. Blessed Anne Catherine Emmerich writes:

> When the Blessed Virgin had reached the age of fourteen and was to be dismissed from the Temple, I saw that the messengers were sent throughout the land and all unmarried men of the line of David were summoned to the Temple (A. Emmerich, 1953, pg.81).

JOSEPH'S DAVIDIC BIRTHRIGHT

In the Book of Genesis, the prophecy of Jacob states that the loss of the Davidic crown would be a sign of the coming of the Messiah.

> The scepter shall not be taken away from Judah, ...
> till he come that is to be sent, and he shall be the
> expectation of nations (Genesis 49:10 DRV).

This removal of authority had already happened by the time Joseph was born into the world, nevertheless, Joseph remained the rightful heir of the kings of Judea. However, in the Divine plan, Joseph was meant to serve the Lord as a worker and to hide and humble himself in domestic life, while at the same time being a nobleman. St. Joseph would have had perfect claim to the throne. St. Peter Julian Eymard and St. Bernardino of Siena comment that though the throne was taken from Joseph's family, he was no less a king because of it:

> Therefore, since Christ was King, of the line of David, He made St. Joseph to be born of this same royal line. He wanted him to be noble, of earthly nobility. In the veins of St. Joseph, therefore, flows the blood of David and Solomon, and of all the noble kings of Judah. If his dynasty still sat on the throne, Joseph would be the heir and would have sat on the throne in his turn. Injustice had expelled his family from the throne to which he had the right. For this he is no less a king, the son of these kings of Judah, the greatest, noblest and richest in the world. Thus, in the census records of Bethlehem, St. Joseph was inscribed and recognized by the Roman governor as the heir of David: therein lies his royal title, which is easily identifiable, and bears the royal signature (P. Eymard, 1948, pg. 60).

> St. Joseph was born of a patriarchal, royal and princely race in a direct line. The Gospel of St. Matthew establishes the direct line of all the fathers from Abraham to the spouse of the Virgin, clearly demonstrating that all patriarchal, royal and princely dignity came together in him (B. Albizensci, 1956, pg. 20).

The Sovereign Lord had deigned to make St. Joseph of royal blood, placing in him all the honour and glory of the House of David. Though St. Joseph's family no longer sat on the throne, he was still a continuation of this nobility. He carried this heritage as though it were a secret between himself and his Lord – a sacred bond between an earthly prince and the Ruler of Heaven and Earth. St. Joseph's royalty was not shown with an outward crown, but one which was hidden within his heart – a heart in which the Lord took great consolation and great delight.

JOSEPH FEELS UNWORTHY

Having previously been made aware of the Virgin Mary by his angel, Joseph would often think of her and contemplate how pure and virtuous she was, and how she was especially favoured and loved by God, but never did it enter his mind that he would be worthy to have her for his wife. Nevertheless, he obeyed the summons to report to the Temple. On his way, he prayed to God not that he be chosen as her husband, but instead that the man chosen be truly worthy of her and pleasing to God. Mother Cecelia Baij reveals St. Joseph's prayer in this regard:

> "My God and my Supreme Good! ... I recognize that I am unworthy to be the one to receive from You so eminent a gift as this Most Holy Virgin Mary, as a spouse and companion. I realize that I have no right to expect it. I am going to this meeting only because it has been so ordered. I beg You to give to this most Holy Virgin a bridegroom who will be worthy of her, and who is fully in accord with Your own heart. But to me, kindly grant an increase of Your grace and love. I place myself entirely in Your hands. May whatever pleases You be always done to me. I desire nothing else than that Your holy will be done in me (C. Baij, 1997, pg. 75, 76)."

CHAPTER 5: THE HOLY ESPOUSALS

This chapter speaks of the divine selection of St. Joseph as the worthy spouse of Mary.

> ... a virgin espoused to a man whose name was Joseph, of the house of David; and the virgin's name was Mary (Luke 1:27 DRV).

The Fathers and Doctors of the Church agree that God Himself predestined and sanctified St. Joseph in order that he would be the husband and upholder of the Blessed Virgin Mary and the father and protector of God the Son – Jesus. Tradition holds that the selection of Joseph as Mary's spouse, predestined by God, was brought out by lot. This recalls the process of the selection of the apostle Matthias in the New Testament.

When the Apostles were trying to find a replacement for Judas Iscariot, the apostle who betrayed Christ, they gathered and prayed to God for a sign of who was to be chosen and they drew lots between them:

> And they prayed and said, "Thou, Lord, who knows the hearts of all, show us which of these two men You have chosen ..." And they drew lots between them and the lot fell upon Matthias (Acts 1:24-26 RSV).

When it came to the selection of St. Joseph, there were gathered a group of young men of the House of David, Joseph among them, one of whom was to be chosen as the husband of Mary. Per tradition, and the saints and mystics of the Church, to discern a suitable husband for Mary, the high priest Zachary, by divine inspiration, recalled how the Israelites rebelled against Moses and Aaron. To convince the Israelites that Aaron was the chosen High Priest, God said to Moses:

"Speak to the people of Israel, and get from them rods, one for each fathers' house, … Write each man's name upon his rod, and write Aaron's name upon the rod of Levi. … And the rod of the man whom I choose shall sprout." Moses spoke to the people of Israel; and all their leaders gave him rods, one for each leader, … twelve rods … and behold, the rod of Aaron for the house of Levi had sprouted and put forth buds, and produced blossoms, and it bore ripe almonds (Numbers 17:1-23 RSV).

Using this example, Zachary told each of the men of the House of David to bring a rod with his name engraved on it, and the man whose rod blossomed would be the chosen husband of Mary. The result was part of the fulfillment of the prophecy of Isaiah:

… and there shall come forth a rod out of the root of Jesse, and a flower shall rise up out of his root. And the spirit of the Lord shall rest upon him (Isaiah 11:1-5 DRV).

The event of the selection of Mary's spouse is revealed by Venerable Maria de Agreda, Blessed Anne Catherine Emmerich, and Mother Cecelia Baij:

Among the number was Joseph … for he was one of the descendants of the royal race of David … He was then thirty-three years of age, handsome and of a pleasing countenance, but also of incomparable modesty … and most saintly in all his inclinations … The Most High spoke to the heart of the high priest, inspiring him to place into the hands of each one of the young men a dry stick, with the command that each ask his Majesty with a lively faith, to single out the one whom He had chosen as the spouse of Mary.

While they were thus engaged in prayer the staff which Joseph held was seen to blossom and at the same time a dove of purest white and resplendent with admirable light, was seen to descend and rest upon the head of the saint (M. Agreda, 1912, p. 576).

As Joseph was about to lay his staff on the altar before the Holy of Holies, a white lily blossomed out of the top ... I saw over him an appearance of light like the Holy Ghost (A. Emmerich, 1953, pg. 83).

Suddenly Joseph saw his branch begin to sprout and become bedecked with snow-white blossoms! Everyone around him was soon staring at this miraculous sign ... All those present now saw a snow-white dove descend from Heaven and settle on the head of Joseph. It was now quite certain that of all the candidates, Joseph was the man of God's choice (C. Baij, 1997, pg. 77).

This tradition of the selection of St. Joseph is still upheld by Christians to this day and in almost every image or statue of St. Joseph he is shown holding his staff which is blossoming flowers (either lilies or spikenard) or just holding the flowers themselves. This is a reminder of his purity, and his worthiness in the eyes of the Heavenly Father to be selected as the spouse of the Mother of God.

Maria de Agreda relates the voice of God in the heart of Joseph and the entrance of the Blessed Virgin Mary:

In the interior of Joseph's heart God spoke: "Joseph, my servant, Mary shall be thy spouse; accept her with attentive reverence, for she is acceptable in my eyes, just and most pure in soul and body ..." Calling her forth for her espousal, the chosen one issued forth like the sun, more resplendent than the moon, and she entered into the presence of all with a countenance more beautiful than that of an angel, incomparable in the charm of her beauty, nobility and grace; and the priests espoused her to the most chaste and holy of men, Saint Joseph (M. Agreda, 1912, p. 576).

Her husband, entrusting his heart to her, has an unfailing prize! She brings him good, and not evil ... She is clothed with strength and dignity and she laughs at the days to come. She opens her mouth in wisdom, and on her tongue, is kindly counsel ... Many are the women of proven worth, but you have excelled them all (Proverbs 31:10-29 NAB)!

NUPTIAL ODE

When reading the beautiful Nuptial Ode in the Book of Psalms, Mary can be easily envisioned saying to her husband:

My heart overflows with a goodly theme; ... You are the most handsome of men; grace is poured upon your lips; therefore, God has blessed you forever. ... you love righteousness and hate wickedness. Therefore, God has anointed you with the oil of gladness beyond your companions (Psalm 45:2-8 NRSV)!

The importance of the espousals between Joseph and Mary is shown in the words of Pope Benedict XVI and Pope Leo XIII:

The espousals between Joseph and Mary are an episode of great importance. Joseph was of the royal line of David and, in virtue of his marriage to Mary, would confer on the Son of the Virgin — on God's Son — the legal title of "Son of David," thus fulfilling the prophecies. The espousals of Joseph and Mary are, because of this, a human event, but determinant in the history of humanity's salvation, in the realization of the promises of God; because of this, it also has a supernatural connotation, which the two protagonists accept with humility and trust (Benedict XVI, 2010).

The dignity of the Mother of God is certainly so sublime that nothing can surpass it; but none the less, since the bond of marriage existed between Joseph and the Blessed Virgin, there can be no doubt that, more than any other person, he approached that super-eminent dignity by which the Mother of God is raised far above all created natures. For marriage is the closest possible union and relationship whereby each spouse mutually participates in the goods of the other.

Consequently, if God gave Joseph as a spouse to the Virgin He assuredly gave him not only as a companion in life, a witness of her virginity, and the guardian of her honour, but also as a sharer in her exalted dignity because of the conjugal tie itself (Leo XIII, 1889).

CHAPTER 6: THE OLD WIDOWER?

This chapter speaks of the false portrayal, held by some, of St. Joseph as an old widower at the time of his espousal to Mary. It also speaks of Joseph's perpetual virginity.

At the time of the holy espousals Joseph was thirty-three years of age and Mary aged fourteen to sixteen years – the mystics Venerable Maria de Agreda, Mother Maria Cecilia Baij, and Blessed Anne Catherine Emmerich reveal this. Through the ages European art has depicted Joseph as an elderly man hunched over his walking stick, or, more commonly in Eastern Nativity icons, as an old man sitting on the ground away from the Virgin Mary and newborn Jesus. In true Russian Orthodox icons St. Joseph is always depicted as being elderly and is never to be holding the Child Jesus or touching the Virgin Mary. He is merely an observer.

The first reason of depicting St. Joseph this way was to explain the "brothers and sisters" of the Lord, mentioned in the Bible (Matthew 12:46). The book known as *The History of Joseph the Carpenter*, which paraphrases the apocryphal book *The Protoevangelium of James*, condemned by Pope Innocent I, states that Joseph was a widower with four sons and two daughters, and married the Virgin Mary when he was roughly seventy-eight years old.

> There was a man whose name was Joseph; he married a wife. Moreover, he begot for himself four sons, namely, and two daughters. Now these are their names — Judas, Justus, James, and Simon. The names of the two daughters were Assia and Lydia. Now when righteous Joseph became a widower ... the lot (to choose a husband for the young Virgin Mary) fell upon the pious old man. He therefore

received Mary, and led her away to his own house … The whole age of Joseph, that righteous old man, was one hundred and eleven years, and the day on which his soul left his body was the twenty-sixth of the month Abib (April). (A. Roberts & J. Donaldson, 1903, pg. 388).

This was a way of justifying the so-called "brothers and sisters" of Jesus. However, all the mystics agree that Joseph had no wife but Mary. The idea of Christ having "brothers and sisters" will be explained in a later chapter.

The second reason for the "elderly Joseph" was to protect the doctrine of the perpetual virginity of Mary. The idea of the Virgin Mary living with a handsome and robust man was not acceptable as it would not be common for a young married couple to remain virgins. Focusing on the physical and not the spiritual, people could not envision this marriage as being without sexual relations unless there was some sort of physical barrier, such as the husband being too old to engage in such actions with his wife. St. Josemaria Escrivá speaks of St. Joseph's youth and strength in a positive way, as not being obstacles to the noble and virginal love he has for Mary:

> I don't agree with the traditional picture of St. Joseph as an old man, even though it may have been prompted by a desire to emphasize the perpetual virginity of Mary. I see him as a strong young man … in the prime of his life and work. You don't have to wait to be old or lifeless to practice the virtue of chastity. Purity comes from love; and the strength and gaiety of youth is no obstacle for noble love. Joseph had a young heart and a young body when he married Mary, when he learned of the mystery of her

divine motherhood, when he lived in her company, respecting the integrity God wished to give the world as one more sign that He had come to share the life of His creatures. Anyone who cannot understand a love like that knows very little of true love and is a stranger to the Christian meaning of chastity (J. Escrivá, 2017, pg. 1&2).

The Bible indicated that the Messiah would be born of a virgin (Isaiah 7:14). Mary herself told the Archangel Gabriel that she was a virgin when he revealed to her that she would conceive a son:

> "How can this be since I am a virgin (Luke 1:34 NRSV)?"

If Mary was not planning to remain a virgin through the course of her marriage, she would not have had to ask "how can this be?" since, naturally, she would conceive the child with Joseph her husband. Again, this will be discussed in a later chapter. St. Jerome, Doctor of the Church, explains the virginal relationship between Joseph and Mary:

> That God was born of a virgin we believe because we read it in the Holy Bible. That Mary consummated marriage after her childbirth we do not believe because we do not read it. Nor do we say this to condemn marriage, for virginity is itself a fruit of marriage, but because there is no license to draw rash conclusions about holy men. For if we wish to take the mere possibility into consideration, we can contend that Joseph had several wives because Abraham and Jacob had several wives and that from these wives, the 'brethren of the Lord' were born, a fiction which most people invent with not so much pious as presumptuous audacity! You say that Mary

47

did not remain a virgin; even more do I claim that Joseph was virginal through Mary, in order that from a virginal marriage a virginal son might be born. For if the charge of fornication does not fall on this holy man, and if it is not written in the Bible that he had another wife, and if he was more of a protector than a husband of Mary, whom he was thought to have as his wife, it remains to assert that he who merited to be called the father of the Lord remained virginal with her (P. Schaff & H. Wace, 2007, pg. 344).

VOW OF CHASTITY

From the earliest days of the Church, the faithful believed in the perpetual virginity of the mother of Jesus. Also, Church traditions fully support that Joseph, being led by the Holy Spirit, chose to offer everything about himself to God and had made a vow of virginity early on in life. Given that he was sanctified by God and given many special graces, this doesn't seem so strange. Venerable Maria de Agreda, Mother Cecelia Baij, St. Francis de Sales and St. John Paul II speak of the virtue of Joseph's virginity:

> Joseph had made and kept the vow of chastity ... and was known for the utmost purity of his life, holy and irreprehensible in the eyes of God and of men. (M. Agreda, 1912, p. 576).

> As he made his promise of perpetual virginity to God, Joseph's heart was filled with an inexpressible joy (C. Baij, 1997, pg. 54).

> How exalted in this virtue of virginity must Joseph have been who was destined by the Eternal Father to be the companion in virginity of Mary! Both had

made a vow to preserve virginity for their entire lives, and it was the Will of God to join them in the bond of a holy marriage (E. Thompson, 1953, pg. 90).

In the Liturgy, Mary is celebrated as "united to Joseph, the just man, by a bond of marital and virginal love." There are two kinds of love here, both of which *together* represent the mystery of the Church - virgin and spouse - as symbolized in the marriage of Mary and Joseph.

Virginity or celibacy for the sake of the Kingdom of God not only does not contradict the dignity of marriage but presupposes and confirms it. Marriage and virginity are two ways of expressing and living the one mystery of the Covenant of God with his people, the Covenant which is a communion of love between God and human beings (John Paul II, 1989).

Joseph gave his gift of virginity to God. This was a holy vow, not because sexual relations are bad and he was abstaining from it, but because he recognized this God-given gift as being so wonderful and intimate that he wanted to offer it and himself entirely to God. This was a selfless act of love.

VIRGINAL TRINITY

God the Father is a virgin who generates the Son in all His goodness; God the Son is a virgin who existed in Heaven without a mother; God the Holy Spirit is a virgin, who proceeds gloriously from the Father and the Son. As the Heavenly Trinity is the first and altogether virgin, so is the second Trinity, on earth. The Earthly Trinity of Jesus, Mary and Joseph mirror the Heavenly Trinity of the Father, Son and Holy Spirit – Jesus (God the Son) connecting the two Trinities. If Jesus is a virgin, and Mary is a virgin, why couldn't Joseph, who would complete this virginal Trinity, be one as they are?

CHAPTER 7: THE MESSENGER

This chapter speaks of the Annunciation to Mary, Joseph's decision to leave Mary and her unborn child, and the Annunciation to Joseph.

> As the cold of snow in the time of harvest, so is a faithful messenger to him that sent him, for he refresheth his soul (Proverbs 25:13, DRV).

After Mary and Joseph were betrothed to one another, the date of their marriage was set, per Church tradition, for January 23. It is believed that the Archangel Gabriel paid homage to the Virgin Mary between the betrothal or *quiddushin,* and the actual marriage ceremony, *nissu'in:*

> "Hail, full of grace, the Lord is with you! Blessed are you among women!" When she heard him, she was troubled at his word, and kept pondering what manner of greeting this was. "Do not be afraid, Mary, for you have found grace with God. Behold, you will conceive ... and will bring forth a son; and you will call his name Jesus. He will be great and will be called the Son of the Most High; and the Lord God will give Him the throne of David ... and of His kingdom there will be no end! ... The Holy Spirit will come upon you and the power of the Most High will overshadow you; and therefore, the Holy One to be born will be called the Son of God (Luke 1:28-36 RSVCE)."

JOURNEY TO THE HOME OF ZECHARIAH AND ELIZABETH

During the period between the engagement and the marriage, Joseph accompanied Mary to visit her relatives Elizabeth, who was pregnant with John the Baptist, and Zechariah. Joseph was still unaware of Mary's pregnancy as she had not yet told him. Though the journey to the hill country of Judea was an arduous one, it also proved to be a joyful one, as Mother Cecelia Baij reveals:

> Before departing, Mary humbled herself by asking Joseph for his blessing and he gave it to her with sincerity and tenderness of heart. ... As they journeyed Joseph asked his spouse to sing some joyful hymns. Mary complied and sang delightfully, praising God. Joseph became completely enraptured thereby, and travelled many miles completely absorbed in God, and entirely alienated from the world of senses (C. Baij, 1997, pg. 100, 101).

JOSEPH ALONE AT NAZARETH

After leaving the Virgin Mary at the house of her relatives, Joseph returned to Nazareth to continue his carpentry. In Mary's absence Joseph had moments of deep loneliness but would then receive visits from one of his angels to console him, as related by Mother Cecelia Baij:

> Since Joseph no longer had Mary's presence to console him when he was weary or lonesome, he would retire to the little room he had set aside for her. There he would kneel and consider his spouse. Then he would begin to weep. ... During this period, Joseph received many visits from one of his angels, who gave him news concerning his spouse. The angel assured him of Mary's support through her prayers and described how she was continually increasing in virtue and grace and love for God. ... Joseph always obtained his greatest consolation when he remained

in her room to pray. There his spirit was quickened and very often enraptured, and he was granted understanding of many of the divine mysteries (C. Baij, 1997, pg. 104, 105).

JOSEPH LEARNS OF MARY'S PREGNANCY

… before they came together, she was found to be with child (Matthew 1:18 RSVCE).

It was when Mary returned to Nazareth that Joseph found out that his virgin-bride was with child. There is debate as to what St. Joseph knew at that time concerning the conception. Some say that the Blessed Virgin made the angelic Annunciation known to him and how the miraculous conception came about. Feeling unworthy of being the husband of holy Mary, and the putative father of the Son of God, Joseph decided to remove himself from this situation with the utmost humility.

Others argue that St. Joseph simply believed Mary to have committed the sin of adultery – that she carried another man's child. Eastern Church tradition says that Joseph was tempted by the devil, being told that Mary was an adulteress and that Joseph was a fool for believing her story. The devil tried to convince Joseph to abandon Mary thereby interfering with God's ultimate plan of salvation. This temptation of Joseph is depicted in many Eastern Nativity icons as he is shown seated on the ground and being approached by the devil who is disguised as an elderly shepherd. On his face is a look of despair which is all too rewarding for the devil.

And still others believe that he was not made aware of the supernatural circumstances of Mary's pregnancy (conception by the Holy Spirit) nor did he suspect that she was an adulteress: He simply did not know what to think – he was baffled by this mystery. The anxiety that penetrated St. Joseph's heart is expressed by Venerable Maria de Agreda:

> The divine pregnancy of Mary had advanced to its fifth month when the most chaste Joseph commenced to notice the condition of the Virgin ... The man of God was wounded to his inmost heart by an arrow of grief ... The principal cause of his grief was the ... most intense love with which he cherished his most faithful spouse ... Besides this, was the certainty of his not having any part in this pregnancy ... The most intimate cause of his sorrow, and which gave him the deepest pain, was the dread of being obliged to deliver over his spouse to the authorities to be stoned, for this was the punishment of an adulteress convicted of the crime:
>
> If a man commits adultery with another man's wife ... both the adulterer and the adulteress must be put to death (Leviticus 20:10).
>
> The heart of Saint Joseph, filled with this painful consideration, found itself, as it were, exposed to the thrusts of many sharp–edged swords, without any other refuge than the full confidence which he had in his spouse ... there was no escape from these tormenting thoughts, and he did not dare to communicate about his grievous affliction with anybody (M. Agreda, 1912, p. 303).

It was time for St. Joseph to make the hardest decision of his life: to leave Mary quietly without shaming her. Though he was a just observer of the law, he would not make the accusation of adultery against her. Venerable Maria De Agreda and Blessed Ann Catherine Emmerich relate:

> Joseph was anxiously debating within himself concerning the proper course of action ... he argued with himself: "I do not find a better way out of these difficulties than to absent myself. I confess that my spouse is most perfect and exhibits nothing but what shows her a saint; but after all she is pregnant, and I cannot fathom the mystery. I do not wish to injure her reputation of holiness by involving her in the punishment of the law; yet at the same time I cannot stand by and witness the consequences of her pregnancy. I will leave her now, and commit myself to the providence of the Lord, who governs me (M. Agreda, 1912, p. 316)."

> St. Joseph noticed from Mary's figure that she was with child and was sore beset by trouble and doubt ... Joseph, though greatly disquieted by what he had perceived, said nothing, but struggled in silence with his doubts. The Blessed Virgin, who had foreseen this trouble, became thoughtful and serious, which only increased St. Joseph's uneasiness. ... Joseph's uneasiness increased to such an extent that he made up his mind to leave her and to disappear in secret (A. Emmerich, 1953, pg. 103).

> ... her husband Joseph, being a just man and unwilling to put her to shame, resolved to send her away quietly (Matthew 1:19 RSVCE).

This situation caused Joseph a lot of heartache. Was their marriage not ordained by God? What of the miracle that announced his selection as the spouse of Mary? Where did this child come from, if not from another man? So many thoughts whirled through Joseph's head as he called out to the Heavens:

> "Hear, O Lord, my voice, with which I have cried to thee: have mercy on me and hear me. My heart hath said to thee: My face hath sought thee: thy face, O Lord, will I still seek. Turn not away thy face from me; decline not in thy wrath from thy servant. Be thou my helper, forsake me not; do not thou despise me, O God my Saviour (Psalm 27:7-9 DRV)!"

THE ANNUNCIATION TO ST. JOSEPH

The Blessed Virgin Mary was heartbroken to see Joseph so wounded by this. She prayed to God to take pity on Joseph, to enlighten him, to ease his suffering. So, being full of mercy and love, the Lord sent the Archangel Gabriel once again to deliver a message:

> But while he thought on these things, behold the angel of the Lord appeared to him in his sleep, saying: Joseph, son of David, fear not to take unto thee Mary thy wife, for that which is conceived in her, is of the Holy Ghost. She will bear a Son; and you shall call His name Jesus, for He will save His people from their sins (Matthew 1:20-22 DRV).

WHY THE ANNUNCIATION TO JOSEPH IN HIS SLEEP?

There are some who are perplexed as to why this great announcement to Joseph took place while he was sleeping rather than while he was awake. The reasons for this are given by Venerable Maria de Agreda:

The first reason is, since Joseph was so prudent and filled with heavenly light, that it was not necessary to convince him by strong evidence to assure him of Mary's dignity and of the mysteries of the Incarnation.

The second reason is, because his trouble had its beginning in seeing with his open eyes the pregnancy of his spouse, that they, having given occasion for suspicion, should be closed in order to see the angelic vision.

The third reason is that it was befitting for the angel deliver this message to him at a time when his senses, which had been scandalized to the point of grief, were suspended, that Joseph be in a state of peace and tranquility of spirit (M. Agreda, 1912, p. 324, 325).

JOSEPH ACCEPTS MARY AND HER UNBORN CHILD

St. Joseph had his own Annunciation in which his anxieties were put at ease as the angel calmed him and told him to have no fear in keeping Mary as his spouse. The Virgin's divine pregnancy and the importance of this child were explained to him as well. Joseph was bestowed with the high honour of not only naming the boy "Jesus," which means "God Saves," but also raising the Son of the Most High as his own son. With these revelations and instructions, the Lord revealed to Joseph that he was indeed worthy for such an important role as being father to the Son of God and spouse of the Mother of God; Joseph was to assume the legitimate rights and position of true father and true husband. God wanted him specifically – not the wealthy man on the hill, not the noble warrior, but the humble carpenter of the line of David.

> And Joseph awoke from his sleep and did as the angel of the Lord commanded him and took Mary as his wife (Matthew 1:24 DRV).

MEN OF DOUBT

In the Old Testament there is a similar story to that of the annunciation to St. Joseph, involving the highly revered forefather Abraham. The message is similar, but the circumstances are different. Abraham is told that his ninety-year-old wife will conceive and bear a child in her old age, who was to become the great man Isaac. Also, in the New Testament, the messenger Gabriel is sent to Zechariah to announce that his elderly wife Elizabeth will bear a son to be named John, the cousin of Jesus. Both Abraham and Zechariah place doubt in the messages given to them, whereas Joseph believes the angel completely:

> Then Abraham fell on his face and laughed, and said in his heart, "Will a child be born to a man one hundred years old? And will Sarah, who is ninety years old, bear a child (Genesis 17:17 NASB)?"

> Zacharias said to the angel, "How will I know this for certain? For I am an old man and my wife is advanced in years (Luke 1:18 NASB)."

Just as unlikely that a one-hundred-year-old man and his ninety-year-old wife would conceive and have a child born to them, so too did it seem impossible for a virgin to conceive. However, unlike father Abraham who laughed at this notion, and Zechariah who doubted, Joseph humbly accepted the divine message that was given to him. He may not have understood completely how this was to be, but for him it did not matter. What mattered was his complete trust in the words of the angel and his surrender to the Divine Will.

> You shall therefore impress these words of mine on your heart and on your soul; and you shall bind them as a sign on your hand, and they shall be as frontals on your forehead (Deuteronomy 11:18 NASB).

As soon as the dream was over, Joseph got up and went to Mary to tell her the news. God had not abandoned him after all! By getting up and acting as he did, St. Joseph had given his *fiat* – his "yes" to cooperating in God's mission, just as the Blessed Virgin Mary had done. By doing this, St. Joseph's mental anguish and spiritual wounds were healed, and his confidence fully mended as he became part of God's redemptive plan. Pope Benedict XVI shares:

> Joseph teaches us that it is possible to love without possessing ... In contemplating Joseph, all men and women can, by God's grace, come to experience healing from their emotional wounds, if only they embrace the plan that God has begun to bring about in those close to Him, just as Joseph entered the work of redemption through Mary and because of what God had already done in her (Benedict XVI, 2009).

PRAISE BETWEEN SPOUSES

St. Joseph pledged his love and commitment to Mary and the unborn Son of God, by promising to be her husband, protector, and that he would accept the Holy Child within her as his own son. The Song of Songs can be imagined as being sung by the two

Blessed Spouses as commitment is renewed, with Joseph adoring the pure and sinless Virgin Mary:

> "O my love, behold thou art fair, thy eyes are as those of doves ... As the lily among thorns, so is my love among the daughters ... Thou art all fair ... and there is not a spot in thee ... my spouse is a garden enclosed ... a fountain sealed up ... Who is she that cometh forth as the morning rising, fair as the moon, bright as the sun? How beautiful art thou ... my dearest (Song of Solomon 1:15, 2:2, 4:7,12, 6:10, 7:6 DRV)!"

And the Holy Virgin replies to Joseph:

> "As the apple tree among the trees of the woods, so is my beloved among the sons. I sat down under his shadow ... He has brought me to his banquet hall and his banner over me is love ... Sustain me ... because I am lovesick ... Let his left hand be under my head and his right hand embrace me ... His appearance is like Lebanon, choice as its cedars, he is altogether lovely. This is my beloved, this is my friend. My beloved is radiant ... he stands out among thousands! His eyes are like doves beside running waters ... His stature is ... imposing as cedars. His mouth is sweetness itself; he is all delight. Such is my beloved (Song of Solomon 2:3-6, 5:10-16 DRV)."

PART TWO: THE VIRGIN FATHER

A righteous man who walks in his integrity — how blessed are his sons after him (Proverbs 20:7 NASB).

CHAPTER 1: ROAD TO FATHERHOOD

This chapter speaks of the census, the journey of Joseph and Mary to Bethlehem, and the importance of Bethlehem to the forthcoming birth of Christ.

As time passed, Joseph and Mary lived a simple but happy life as they waited with joy for the birth of their promised son. They carried the secret that Joseph wasn't the child's biological father but knew that it wouldn't keep him from being a *true* father. He would be excited, as most men would be, to tell the whole world that he was going to be a father! Mary would marvel at Joseph's anticipation and acceptance in fulfilling God's Will in naming and rearing the child as his own. She no doubt treasured these mysteries in her Immaculate Heart – as she treasured the other mysteries present in her life.

> Mary treasured all these things, pondering them in her heart (Luke 2:19 NASB).

THE CENSUS

As months went by the Holy Child grew within His tabernacle, the womb of the Blessed Virgin, and His time was drawing near. Soon He would be in Bethlehem, where King David was born, where Joseph was born, and where He too would be born into the world. It was during the ninth month that a census was ordered by Caesar Augustus, which meant that everyone had to return to the lands of their forefathers to register and be counted.

> And Joseph went up from Galilee, out of the city of Nazareth into Judea, to the city of David, which is called Bethlehem: because he was of the house and family of David, to be enrolled with Mary his espoused wife, who was with child (Luke 2:4-5 DRV).

THE IMPORTANCE OF BETHLEHEM

It is important to note the significance of Bethlehem being the birthplace of both St. Joseph and our Lord Jesus for three reasons:

The first reason: Jesus was foreseen to be a descendent of the great King David and therefore Joseph, His earthly father, would have to have been of the House of David who comes from Bethlehem.

> And when thy days be fulfilled, and thou shalt sleep with thy fathers, I will set up thy seed after thee ... and I will establish his kingdom. He shall build a house for my name, and I will stablish the throne of his kingdom forever (2 Samuel 7:12-13 NIV).

The Second reason: Joseph's reporting to Bethlehem at that time, which resulted in the Virgin Mary giving birth to the Messiah there, also added to the fulfillment of the prophecy of Micah which announced that this place would bring our Lord to the world:

> Thou Bethlehem, art a little one among the thousands of Juda: out of thee shall he come forth unto me that is to be the ruler in Israel: and his going forth is from the beginning, from the days of eternity (Micah 5:1-2 DRV).

The third reason: the word Bethlehem, *Bet Lehem* in Hebrew, means "House of Bread" and this is of tremendous significance since Jesus Christ called Himself the "Living Bread":

> "I am the living bread which came down from Heaven. If any man eats of this bread, he shall live for ever; and the bread that I will give, is my flesh, for the life of the world (John 6:51 DRV)."

Just as the Joseph of the Old Testament provided bread for his brothers when they sought him in hunger (Genesis 41:55-57, 42:25), how much more did St. Joseph in Bethlehem present to us the true, *living* bread, Jesus Christ. He held this life-giving bread in his folded arms and guarded it as a storehouse, but eager to nourish mankind. Thus, he is praised by 15th century author Wilhelm Nakatenus in his Officium Parvum Sancte Ioseph:

> Hail glory of the patriarchs, steward of God's holy Church, who didst preserve the Bread of Life and the Wheat of the Elect (F. Lasance, 1904, pg. 591).

JOURNEY OF FIVE DAYS

St. Joseph had to report to Bethlehem, the birthplace of King David, which is roughly 130 kilometers (80 miles) south of Nazareth, where he and Mary were living. To reach Bethlehem they would have to cross the rough terrain of Samaria into Judea. Though Joseph would be saddened to not have Mary by his side, he was also hesitant to bring her along since she was soon to give birth. Concerning this, Venerable Maria de Agreda reveals the words of St. Joseph to the Blessed Virgin:

> "My Queen, if God has not revealed to you otherwise, it seems to me that I should make the journey to Bethlehem alone. Yet, although this order to report refers only to the heads of families, I dare not leave you without assistance, nor would I have a moment's peace away from you; for my heart could not come to any rest without seeing you. However, your delivery is too fast approaching to ask you to go with me to Bethlehem, and I do not want to place you in any risk (M. Agreda, 1912, p. 375)."

And the words of the Blessed Virgin to her spouse:

> "My spouse and my master, I will accompany thee with much pleasure, and we will make this journey in the name of the Lord. Relying on His protection and assistance in our necessities and labours, we will proceed with confidence (M. Agreda, 1912, p. 377, 378)."

To be sure, St. Joseph and the Blessed Virgin prayed on it asking for God's guidance in the matter. It was revealed to Mother Cecelia Baij that an angel was sent to Joseph with the answer:

> During the night, Joseph's angel appeared to him and told him that what he had decided upon with his spouse was in accordance with the will of God, and that he should proceed to carry it out. This message of the angel made Joseph feel completely satisfied (C. Baij, 1997, pg. 144).

CORPUS CHRISTI PROCESSION

This journey to Bethlehem was the first Corpus Christi (Latin for "Body of Christ") procession to take place, except in this case the Body of Christ was enclosed in His mother's womb, rather than being exposed for veneration by the faithful. Mary's mantle was the canopy over the Hidden Jesus who is our Bread of Life, and Joseph's sandal prints on the dusty earth were as palms and petals laid out for the Lord to tread on. First instituted by Jesus Himself at the Last Supper, the Eucharist has been revered by the Roman Catholic Church and given a feast day of celebration, the Feast of Corpus Christi. Traditionally on the feast day of Corpus Christi, a consecrated Host is carried in procession under the shade of a canopy for the veneration of the faithful, as flowers and palm branches are strewn upon the ground, making a pathway for the real presence of Jesus in the Eucharist.

ONWARD

The journey to Bethlehem surely took its toll on Joseph's feet, but with each step he knew that he was moving closer to fulfilling what the angel had told him regarding the birth of Christ. The heat and terrain were at times barely tolerable, but Joseph would no doubt comfort our Lady as best as he could, as they journeyed toward their destination. Joseph's first action, whenever they rested by the way or stop for the night, was to make ready a comfortable place for the Blessed Virgin to sit and rest. Blessed Anne Catherine Emmerich reveals Joseph's disposition during the journey:

> Joseph spoke so comfortingly to the Blessed Virgin, he is so good, and so sorry that the journey is difficult (A. Emmerich, 1953, pg. 106).

NO VACANCY

Arriving in Bethlehem and searching for shelter, the holy couple was rejected by the innkeepers and residents. The town of Bethlehem was full of visitors coming to register for the census which made for overcrowding and no vacancies. Joseph began to feel desperate at not finding a place to stay. To add to the anxiousness, the time for Jesus to be born was at hand.

Finally, he went to one last house and begged for help. The owner apologized and stated that he too was out of room, and the only unoccupied spot was a cave just outside of town, which the animals used. Joseph accepted the man's suggestion, feeling relieved but also ashamed. Joseph felt as though he had failed, that he could not do better for his beloved, and his most pure heart was pierced with sorrow. Venerable Maria de Agreda relates:

> It was nine o'clock at night when the most faithful Joseph, full of bitter and heartrending sorrow, returned to his spouse and said: "My sweetest Lady, my heart is broken with sorrow at the thought of not being able to shelter thee as thou deserve (M. Agreda, 1912, p. 388, 389)."

One traditional prayer, "Thirty Days' Prayer to St. Joseph", refers to the weariness of St. Joseph in Bethlehem:

> I ask my favour by the weariness and suffering you endured when you found no shelter at the inn of Bethlehem for the Holy Virgin, nor a house where the Son of God could be born. Then, being everywhere refused, you had to allow the Queen of Heaven to give birth to the world's Redeemer in a cave.

Not only was our Lord's birth in Bethlehem predicted in the Old Testament, but also the surroundings in which He would was to be born were envisioned: The rejection of the townspeople and the presence of animals at His birth. In the Gospel of St. Matthew an appropriate phrase can also be applied to the rejection in Bethlehem:

> The ox knoweth his owner, and the ass his master's crib: but Israel hath not known me, and my people hath not understood (Isaiah 1:3 DRV).

> For I was hungry, and you gave me not to eat. I was thirsty, and you gave me not to drink. I was a stranger, and you took me not in (Matthew 25:42-43 DRV).

CHAPTER 2: THE HUMBLE CRIB

This chapter speaks of the ecstasy of St. Joseph, the Nativity of Christ, and the homage paid to Him by the poor shepherds.

> The greater thou art, the more humble thyself in all
> things, and thou shalt find grace before God (Sirach
> 3:20 DRV).

At the entrance to the cave, St. Joseph shined his lantern to see what lay inside. He crept in and searched for an ideal spot for Mary to lie down. In the far corner, there was a pile of straw and for the most part it was clean. He then went back to his wife and helped her down from the donkey's back. He unloaded all their belongings and made a bed out of straw with blankets stretched out over top. He then escorted Mary into her temporary bedchamber, and she assured him that this would do just fine.

THE ECSTASY OF ST. JOSEPH

A seldom asked question is, "was Joseph present at the moment of Christ's birth?" Some Eastern Rites believe that he went out looking for a midwife and, when he returned with one, the child had already been born. However, according to Venerable Maria de Agreda and St. Faustina Kowalska, St. Joseph was indeed present at Christ's birth and it has been revealed that blessed Joseph was enraptured in a holy ecstasy:

> St. Joseph retired to a corner of the entrance, where
> he began to pray. He was immediately elevated into
> an ecstasy. In it was shown him all that passed
> during that night in this blessed cave; for he did not
> return to consciousness until his heavenly spouse
> called him. Such was the sleep which St. Joseph
> enjoyed in that night, more exalted and blessed than

that of Adam in paradise ... Joseph issued from his ecstasy and, on being restored to consciousness, the first sight of his eyes was the divine Child in the arms of the Virgin Mother reclining against her sacred countenance and breast. There he adored Him in profoundest humility and in tears of joy he kissed His feet in great joy and admiration (M. Agreda, 1912, p. 396).

I saw the stable of Bethlehem filled with great radiance. The Blessed Virgin, all lost in the deepest of love, was wrapping Jesus in swaddling clothes, but Joseph was still asleep (in his ecstasy). Only after the Mother of God put Jesus in the manger, did the light of God awaken Joseph, who also prayed (F. Kowalska, 2005, pg. 318).

Though St. Joseph was experiencing an ecstasy of the Nativity, he was still present and, once he was awakened from it, he was the first man to adore the Divine Child. He held the Infant in his arms and kissed His little feet in adoration. Joseph was full of joy as his wife had just given birth to Love Incarnate, the Saviour, and a New Adam for the world! Venerable Maria de Agreda reveals the moment in which St. Joseph first received the divine Infant into his arms:

When for the first time the Blessed Virgin placed the infant God in Joseph's arms, most holy Mary said to him: "My husband and my helper, receive in thy arms ... the Treasure of the Eternal Father and participate in this blessing of the human race."

Her most faithful husband humbled himself and answered: "My lady and my spouse, how can I, being so unworthy, presume to hold in my arms God

Himself, in whose presence tremble the pillars of Heaven?"

St. Joseph's desire of holding the infant God and his reverential fear of Him caused in Joseph heroic acts of love, faith, humility and profoundest reverence. Trembling with discreet fear he fell on his knees to receive Him from the hands of His most holy mother, while sweetest tears of joy and delight flowed from his eyes. The divine Infant looked at him caressingly and at the same time renewed his inmost soul (M. Agreda, 1912, p. 425).

Words cannot truly express the magnitude of this event in history. Salvation was given to the world in this Child! The choirs of angels rejoiced at the birth with the night sky illuminated as if it were day! Mankind had received its salvation!

And I heard as it were the voice of a great multitude, and as the voice of many waters, and as the voice of great thunders, saying: Alleluia ... Let us be glad and rejoice and give glory to Him (Apocalypse 19:6-7 DRV).

Praise, O servants of the Lord, praise the name of the Lord. Blessed be the name of the Lord, from this time forth and forever. From the rising of the sun to its setting the name of the Lord is to be praised. The Lord is high above all nations; His glory is above the heavens (Psalm 113:1-4 NASB).

PATERNAL AUTHORITY

On this most holy of nights, Joseph entered the nobility of fatherhood and his paternal title of Virgin-Father was far more superior to simply being a legal guardian or foster-father. Jesus, being conceived by the Holy Spirit, was the crowning splendor of the virginal espousals of St. Joseph and the Blessed Virgin Mary. He wished to humble Himself by being born of a woman and by submitting Himself to the paternal authority of His chosen father Joseph, thereby establishing a true relationship between father and son. Joseph assumed all responsibility and honour befitting a father and it was Jesus who willed that he be master over Himself and His Blessed Mother, giving St. Joseph his rightful place as the head of the Holy Family. Though Christ is King, and our Lady is Queen, Joseph has sovereign authority over both as the established father-head of the family. St. Augustine of Hippo, Doctor of the Church, praises Joseph's fatherhood thusly:

> Oh, holy Joseph! You receive from Mary through the Holy Spirit, God's own Son as your son, by a means of conception as legitimate as it was sublime. Your virginity, and that of Mary, is thereby far from being marred. Instead, and rightly so, it is precisely because of your perfect virginity that your spouse Mary, the Virgin of virgins, becomes the Mother of God! It is due to you, as well as to herself, and therefore, you are also truly a father (O. Staudinger, 1997, pg. 385).

SHEPHERDS' HOMAGE

The first dignitaries to pay homage to the Infant King and his parents were not of the elite or noble classes of society, but rather the lowly shepherds from nearby. Shepherds were disregarded people and they were very low in society. These shepherds, keeping watch over their flocks, were granted the esteemed privilege of receiving a visitation from the angels of the Lord.

They received the message that the promised Messiah was born, and they were invited, above all others, to behold Him.

> But the angel said to them, "Do not be afraid; for behold, I bring you good news of great joy which will be for all the people; for today in the city of David there has been born for you a Saviour, who is Christ the Lord. This will be a sign for you: you will find a baby wrapped in cloths and lying in a manger." And suddenly there appeared with the angel a multitude of the heavenly host praising God and saying, "Glory to God in the highest, and on earth peace among men with whom He is pleased." ... So they came in a hurry and found their way to Mary and Joseph, and the baby as He lay in the manger (Luke 2:10-16 DRV).

St. Joseph was glad to welcome these visitors and the fact that they were lowly shepherds made no difference to him as he invited the shepherds to approach and gaze upon the newborn. How small and fragile was the Son of God, lying there in sweet repose.

> Shepherds came to adore the newly born Saviour. Joseph was greatly surprised to see them come with such fervor and devotion to adore the Infant in such a miserable place ... His love for poverty was increased ... for he saw what a special regard the Saviour had for this virtue. Joseph noticed how joyfully the Divine Infant, this God of wisdom and majesty, received the visiting shepherds (C. Baij, 1997, pg. 154, 155).

The royal child was not wrapped in sparkling clean silk or velvet robes, but in humble swaddling clothes and Joseph's cloak. Still, the shepherds adored this child who would one day be known as the Good Shepherd and take His place as King of Heaven and Earth. The shepherds revealed to Joseph and Mary the message of the angel and the vision they beheld in the sky, and they treasured this encounter with the Holy Family, where Mary and Joseph felt the same way.

> When they had seen this, they made known the statement which had been told them about this Child. And all who heard it wondered at the things which were told them by the shepherds. But Mary treasured all these things, pondering them in her heart. The shepherds went back, glorifying and praising God for all that they had heard and seen, just as had been told them (Luke 2:17-20 NASB).

CHAPTER 3: FIRST DROPS OF BLOOD

This chapter speaks of St. Joseph's first official act as a father, the circumcision and naming of Jesus.

> This is My covenant, which you shall keep, between Me and you and your descendants after you: every male among you shall be circumcised. And you shall be circumcised in the flesh of your foreskin, and it shall be the sign of the covenant between Me and you. And every male among you who is eight days old shall be circumcised throughout your generations (Genesis 17:10-12).

Eight days after the birth of a son, the Law required that he be circumcised. This rite was prescribed by God to Abraham as a sign of His close union with His people. The circumcision of a son was not just a "procedure" back then, but a solemn yet joyful occasion. This meaningful ceremony was fulfilling the Jews' part of their Covenant with God. This sacred rite was so family oriented that it did not even have to take place at the Temple. In fact, they did not even need a priest; it could be done by the boy's father. Beginning in the fourth century, the term "Mohel" was used to identify one who performs circumcisions.

ST. JOSEPH VS. THE PRIEST

In the Gospel of St. Luke, we are not told who circumcised Jesus, whether it was Joseph or if he set out to find a priest to perform the ceremony. Originally the task was given over to the father as in the case of Abraham who circumcised both Ishmael and Isaac. Over time priests could assume this task.

In the earliest and most popular depictions of the circumcision of Christ, it is shown to be performed by what looks to be a priest, with St. Joseph and our Lady standing by. They would have the honour of bestowing upon their son the name given by the angel of the Lord:

> "... and thou shalt call His name Jesus. For he shall save His people from their sins (Matthew 1:21 DRV)."

According to Blessed Anne Catherine Emmerich and Venerable Maria de Agreda, Jesus was circumcised by a priest in the cave of Bethlehem, not at the Temple.

> The circumcision took place eight days after the birth of our Lord. Joseph had gone to Bethlehem and returned with three priests. The circumcision was performed in the cave. The Infant Jesus wept loudly after the sacred ceremony, and I saw that He was given back to St. Joseph who comforted Him (A. Emmerich, 1953, pg. 132).

> The priest came to the cave of the Nativity, where the incarnate Word awaited him. To show as much exterior reverence for the sacred rite of circumcision as was possible in that place, St. Joseph lit two wax candles. ... The priest then circumcised the Child, the true God and man. (M. Agreda, 1912, p. 447, 448).

THREE OFFERINGS

At the circumcision of Jesus, St. Joseph's heart would offer three hidden sacrifices to the Heavenly Father:

The first sacrifice would be the Infant Jesus, though entirely sinless and pure, assuming the degradation of a sinner. He did this by submitting Himself to the rite of circumcision which was instituted as a form of remedy to make peace with the sinner and the Lord. St. Joseph did not have to submit his son to this, since Jesus Himself had no original sin in Him, but out of humility he abided by the Law. Joseph offered up the humility of the Divine Child.

> He made Him who knew no sin to be sin on our behalf, so that we might become the righteousness of God in Him (2 Corinthians 5:21 NASB).

The second offering of St. Joseph was the willingness to allow Christ to suffer the physical pain of the circumcision. This first cut into the tender flesh of Jesus would be His first physical suffering at the hands of another, but with St. Joseph there to comfort Him. Years later at His Passion, Jesus would not be granted consolation during His pain until He breathed His last. He would be helpless and without comfort.

> Insults have broken my heart, so that I am in despair.
> I looked for pity, but there was none; and for comforters, but I found none (Psalm 69:20 NRSVCE).

The third sacrifice at this event would be the shedding of blood, fully displaying the human side of our Lord. St. Joseph would make the first offering of the Most Precious Blood in reparation for the many offences committed against our Lord.

> For this is My blood of the new testament, which shall be shed for many unto remission of sins (Matthew 26:28 DRV).

After this sorrowful course, the heart of Joseph would now be infused with joy as he had just fulfilled his first official act as a father in Jewish society. Since the beginning of time Joseph was chosen, just as Mary was, to play an important role in the history of mankind. Joseph was the first man to utter the name of our

Saviour, his lips having the honour of pronouncing the Most Holy Name of Jesus! How the heavens must have rejoiced at the moment the name of Salvation was spoken! The Bible mentions the circumcision and naming of Jesus and Mother Cecelia Baij gives her account too:

> And after eight days were accomplished, that the child should be circumcised, His name was called Jesus, which was called by the angel, before He was conceived in the womb (Luke 2:21 DRV).

> Joseph stood by attentively during the procedure, gazing steadfastly at the Infant with love and sympathy. Joseph was asked what name should be given to the Child. In his humility Joseph waited for the Mother of God to make the announcement first. By God's Will it happened that they pronounced the name of "Jesus" together. Heaven bowed down at the pronouncement of this name, with all the blessed spirits rendering their homage (C. Baij, 1997, pg. 160).

HUMAN AND DIVINE

Though the circumcision of Jesus was only briefly mentioned in the Bible, it is very important to take notice of this event, not only reminding us of God's presence with His people, but also to prove the reality of His taking on our human nature. In the year 70 A.D. the Docetist heresy was running rampant, denouncing the human nature of Christ, claiming that His body was an illusion and not real flesh and blood, therefore not physically dying for our sins. This belief has always been the antithesis of Christianity, being condemned as heresy by the Council of Jerusalem.

Jesus being God-made-man is human since His body was formed in the womb of the Blessed Mother, while still retaining His divinity. If the Infant Jesus did not take on human flesh, then how could St. Joseph have taken Him to be circumcised? The priest himself cut the foreskin of the Divine Infant and, if His flesh was just an illusion, how could the circumcision have gone through? If one denies the human aspect of Jesus, then one is also denying that Christ could suffer and die for the salvation of mankind — the Passion of Jesus would have no merit.

THE DIVINITY AND HUMANITY OF CHRIST

In many Eastern icons, Jesus is depicted as holding up His right hand and giving the sign of peace. He holds up His index and middle finger side by side and folds in His thumb and remaining fingers. In these images, Jesus appears to be blessing the viewer, but there is also a deeper meaning to the arrangement of His fingers.

The three folded fingers (little finger, ring and thumb) represent the Holy Trinity: The Father, The Son and The Holy Spirit. The three fingers coming together and touching as one represent the total unity of the Holy Trinity, as one God in three Persons. Jesus is the Second Person of the Holy Trinity, the Son.

The two fingers set apart in the appearance of blessing, or giving the sign of peace, represents the two natures of Christ; He is fully God and fully man. This is also where the Blessed Virgin Mary received her holy title "Mother of God", Theotokos (God-Bearer), since Jesus is God.

The circumcision proves, at the early age of eight days, that God literally took on human flesh in the womb of the Blessed Virgin. Joseph, in exercising his paternal authority by submitting Jesus to this rite of circumcision, has shown that the Infant Jesus is indeed God-made-man.

> And the Word was made flesh, and dwelt among us, (and we saw His glory, the glory as it were of the Only Begotten of the Father,) full of grace and truth (John 1:14 DRV).

Soon after, St. Joseph set out to register his family per the census of Caesar Augustus. Joseph would have the honour of pronouncing the names of his Blessed Spouse Mary, as well as his own saintly name, but most importantly the Most Holy Name of Jesus. To Joseph no name would be sweeter than that of his most treasured gift, his only son.

CHAPTER 4: A FAMILY AFFAIR

This chapter speaks of another defense of the virginity of Joseph and Mary, and the "first-born" issue.

"BROTHERS" OF THE LORD

Chapter 6 of Part 1 introduced the issue of the virginity of St. Joseph. Since Joseph vowed his virginity to God, who were the "brothers" of the Lord mentioned in the Gospel of St. Matthew and in the Acts of the Apostles?

> While He was still speaking to the crowds, behold, His mother and brothers were standing outside, seeking to speak to Him (Matthew 12:46 NASB).

> These all with one mind were continually devoting themselves to prayer, along with the women, and Mary the mother of Jesus, and with His brothers (Acts 1:14 NASB).

In the Roman Catholic Church, as well as some Protestant denominations, Mary is known as the "Blessed Virgin". When referring to her as such, the belief that she was a virgin before the birth of Christ as well as after – throughout the course of her life, is affirmed. St. Joseph is also seen as virginal and is referred to, in the Divine Praises, as Mary's "Most Chaste Spouse". There are those who believe that the holy couple later had children whom Scripture refers to as the "brethren of the Lord." In the New Testament, the "brothers" and "sisters" of the Lord are mentioned in the following places: Matthew 12:46-50 & 13:55-56, Mark 3:31-34, Luke 8:19-21, John 2:12 & 7:3 and Acts 1:14.

In the Holy Bible the word "brother" ("adelphos" in Greek) has a wide range of meanings and does not only mean a literal, biological, brother, but casts its net over a wide range of meanings. The Old Testament shows us that the word "brother" could refer to any male relative including cousin, nephew, or other kinsmen, friends, allies etc...

> **Genesis 14:14** Lot is referred to as Abraham's brother though in actuality he was Abraham's nephew.

> **Genesis 29:15** Jacob is called the brother of his uncle Laban.

> **1 Chronicles 23:22** Kish (Cis) and Eleazar were the sons of Mahli. Kis (Cis) had sons of his own, but Eleazar had only daughters. These daughters married their "brethren," the sons of Kish (Cis). These "brethren" were their cousins, not their biological brothers.

> **Jeremiah 34:9** Jeremiah refers to not keeping fellow Jews as slaves. These slaves are referred to as his "brothers".

ANNUNCIATION TO A PERPETUAL VIRGIN

At the Annunciation to Mary in the New Testament, when the Archangel Gabriel announced to her that she would conceive a son, she asked him in all humility:

> "How can this be since I am a virgin (Luke 1:34 NRSV)?"

As previously revealed, Mary had made a vow of virginity – even in marriage. If she had not made this vow, she would have taken the angel's words to mean that she and Joseph would produce a son. If she had not vowed her virginity to God, she would not have asked how this was to come about. Though she and St. Joseph were to be married, she told the angel that she did not "know man", that she did not and would not be having a sexual relationship with her spouse. If this was not the case, there would be no reason for her to state that she was a virgin, since naturally she would have given her virginity to her husband to conceive the son of whom the angel spoke.

Another example that could support the only-child story is shown in the Gospel of St. Luke. In this Gospel an event in the late childhood of Jesus is revealed:

> Now His parents went to Jerusalem every year at the Feast of the Passover. And when He became twelve, they went up there according to the custom of the Feast; and as they were returning, after spending the full number of days, the boy Jesus stayed behind in Jerusalem. But His parents were unaware of it, but supposed Him to be in the caravan, and went a day's journey; ... When they did not find Him, they returned to Jerusalem looking for Him. Then, after three days they found Him in the Temple (Luke 2:41-47 NASB).

In this account, Jesus is almost a man in the eyes of the law, for thirteen is the age at which a Jewish boy reaches manhood. Joseph and Mary had now been husband and wife for twelve years, and yet Jesus is their only child mentioned. Surely if they had not made vows of virginity, they would have had other children besides Jesus by then.

> ... and they began looking for Him among their relatives and acquaintances. When they did not find Him, they returned to Jerusalem looking for Him. Then, after three days they found Him in the Temple,

sitting in the midst of the teachers, both listening to them and asking them questions. And all who heard Him were amazed at His understanding and His answers. ... and His mother said to Him, "Son, why have You treated us this way? Behold, Your father and I have been anxiously looking for You (Luke 2:44-50 NASB)."

The "brothers and sisters" of Christ would have been mentioned by now, and when would be more appropriate to mention them than at a family pilgrimage to Jerusalem? Their extended family is mentioned but no reference is made to "brothers" or "sisters" here. The Holy Bible would have stated that "the boy Jesus was not among His brothers and sisters, nor among His relatives," however it does not.

ST. JOSEPH'S NEPHEWS

Surely the four "brothers" of Jesus spoken of in the Bible would have been mentioned at this family event in Jerusalem, but they were not. According to early Church tradition Joseph had a male relative, (referred to as his brother or cousin), named Cleophas who was also wed to a woman named Mary. This Mary was the mother of James, Joses, Judas, and Simon who are all referred to as the "brothers" of Jesus. Mary is a sister (cousin) to the Blessed Virgin Mary.

> Now there stood by the cross of Jesus, His mother, and His mother's sister, Mary of Cleophas, and Mary Magdalene (John 19:25 DRV).

> Is not this the carpenter, the son of Mary, the brother of James, and Joseph, and Jude, and Simon? Are not

also his sisters here with us? And they were scandalized in regard of him (Mark 6:3 DRV).

"HE KNEW HER NOT ... UNTIL"

In the Holy Bible the use of the word "until" implies that a certain act will or will not happen up until the point of time given. It does not imply that the act will then occur, or cease to be, after the point of time given.

An argument used to denounce the perpetual virginity of St. Joseph and the Blessed Virgin Mary is the passage found in the first chapter of the Gospel of St. Matthew:

> And Joseph rising up from sleep, did as the angel of the Lord had commanded him, and took unto him his wife. And he knew her not until she brought forth her firstborn son: and he called his name Jesus (Matthew 1:24-25 DRV).

In applying the same reasoning for Joseph not having sexual relations with Mary *until* she gave birth, one would also have to say that the daughter of Saul had no children *until* she was dead, meaning she had children after she died, which is nonsensical.

> Therefore, Michal the daughter of Saul had no child until the day of her death (2 Samuel 6:23 WBT).

If one applied the reasoning to Timothy, then St. Paul is instructing Timothy to read scripture, preach, and teach, but is to stop all of that when St. Paul arrives. This is not so.

> Until I come, give attention to the public reading of Scripture, to exhortation and teaching (1 Timothy 4:13 NASB).

85

In applying the reasoning that there were no sexual relations between Joseph and Mary *until* she gave birth, the scripture quote below would reveal that Christ must reign *until* He conquers His enemies but must not reign after that. This is false.

> 1 Corinthians 15:25: For He (Christ) must reign until He has put all His enemies under His feet (1 Corinthians 15:25 NASB).

"BEHOLD THY MOTHER"

Another, more obvious, example is given at the Crucifixion of the Lord. It is evident that Mary had no other children because while her only Son was hanging on the cross, bruised and bleeding, He felt compelled to entrust her into the care of His Beloved Apostle, John. St. Joseph died before Christ entered public ministry, so it would be up to his children to take her in. Why would Jesus give his mother to St. John if He had brothers or sisters to take care of her? Why were His brothers and sisters not at the foot of the cross with their mother?

Is one led to believe that these sons and daughters refused their mother in her hour of need? It does not make sense. So, feeling responsible for His mother's well-being, Christ gave her to His closest companion to watch over. Even in the excruciating pain of His crucifixion, He cared enough to look after His mother till the very end.

> When Jesus therefore had seen His mother and the disciple standing whom He loved, He saith to His mother: Woman, behold thy son. After that, He saith to the disciple: Behold thy mother. And from that hour, the disciple took her to his own. ... And bowing His head, He gave up the ghost (John 19:26-30 DRV).

One might argue that this example is not enough to suggest that Jesus was an only child. To be crucified was the most shameful way to die, and perhaps therefore Jesus' so-called brothers were not at the foot of the cross with their mother. It can be noted that not even His apostles were present, except for John the Beloved. Where were His apostles and friends? They might have been ashamed to be associated with the crucifixion scene – as would His brothers. Still, if Jesus had brothers or sisters, He would not have needed to give His mother into the care of His Beloved Apostle, regardless of whether they were at the foot of the cross. Why would His brothers abandon not only Him, but their mother as well? If we take the "brother" references literally, then out of four possible brothers, would not one of them support their mother? Would all four abandon her?

"FIRST-BORN" ISSUE

There are some who claim that to be called Mary's "first-born", Jesus would have had a sibling born after Him. The claim is made that Christ could not be a "first-born" unless other children were born to Joseph and Mary afterward.

> And she brought forth her firstborn son and wrapped Him up in swaddling clothes (Luke 2:7 DRV).

Using this as an argument shows lack of knowledge of the ways of the ancient Jewish people and how they used that term. In Exodus 13:2 and Numbers 3:12 the child who opened the womb was the first-born and, under the Law of Moses, was to be sanctified, as previously mentioned.

Were the parents required to wait until a second son was born before being allowed to officially call their first son the "firstborn"? Not so. The first son born of a marriage was always referred to as the "first-born" regardless of whether he was an only child.

Why is it so hard for some to believe that the Virgin Mary was in fact a virgin all her life or the same for St. Joseph? God can do whatever He pleases, so why is it so impossible for some to believe that He handcrafted such pure souls as those of Joseph and Mary? His Son Jesus Christ healed the sick, brought the dead back to life, walked on water, rose from the grave, and after forty days ascended to Heaven!

Another hard-hitting example of God's power: He created the universe – all which is seen and unseen! So why should this issue of virginity be so hard for some to believe? Not even the Holy Bible can contain all of God's mysteries and what He has wrought. Why do people try to limit the works of God, by being too proud to have faith in some of His more mysterious works?

> And Jesus beholding, said to them: With men this is impossible: but with God all things are possible (Matthew 19:26 DRV).

> For My thoughts are not your thoughts: nor your ways My ways, saith the Lord (Isaiah 55:8 DRV).

CHAPTER 5: EPIPHANY

This chapter speaks of the Magi of the East paying homage to the Infant Jesus.

Nations will come to Your light, and kings to the brightness of Your rising (Isaiah 60:3 NASB).

Just as Jesus had been revealed to the Jews by way of the shepherds at His crib, so too He was revealed to the Gentiles by means of the infamous "Three Kings" or "Wise Men." As early as 361 A.D., Christians fixed the date of January 6 to be the feast day of the Epiphany, commemorating the Visitation of the Magi (Persian wise men or astrologers) to adore the Infant Jesus. This encounter was to be the revelation of Christ to all nations, as they represented the non-Jewish people of the world.

VISITORS FROM THE EAST

According to the Gospel of St. Matthew the Wise Men of the East came to Bethlehem to pay homage to the newborn King of the Jews. Since three gifts were given to the baby Jesus from the Magi, it has always been assumed that there were three Wise Men sometimes called the "Three Kings of the East". The Bible does not give their names, but tradition as early as the 6th century does: Gaspar (sometimes Caspar or Jaspar), Melchior, and Balthasar. As for where they travelled from, we are only told that they "came from the East", but traditionally they were held to be from Persia, as their earliest depictions in art show them in Persian costume.

Now after Jesus was born in Bethlehem of Judea in the days of Herod the king, magi from the east arrived in Jerusalem (Matthew 2:1 NASB).

A CONTROVERSIAL SIGN

The Magi, also known as the Wise Men, were following a sign in the sky—a bright and unusual star—which guided them to Bethlehem. This star, and the men who followed it, have been the topic of debate for some, as there are those who claim that this star was the work of the devil, most notably the religious group "Jehovah's Witnesses." Their reasoning behind this claim is that since they were astrologers, they were to be condemned rather than celebrated. They see the arrival of the astrologers as something diabolical since the Bible condemns sorcery and astrology in such books as Deuteronomy 18:10-11 and Isaiah 47:13-14.

Also, the fact that the star followed by the Magi led them directly to the evil King Herod does not help their case. The Wise Men spoke to the king regarding the birth of Jesus (the prophesied King of the Jews) and because of this he later sought to kill the child. Had the Wise Men not seen the star and followed it, King Herod might not have been alerted to the birth of this "King of the Jews" whom he saw to be a threat to his power.

Afterwards, Herod would deploy his soldiers into the town of Bethlehem to destroy all the male children under the age of two years, in the hopes that one of them would be the newborn king. Though this would be a sorrowful event in history, these slain Innocents would become the first martyrs who shed their blood for Christ.

In the end, most Christian denominations believe the star was a sign to be celebrated as it served as a guide to lead the pagan gentiles to the true God. However, the "Jehovah's Witnesses" still believe that this star, and the Wise Men, were part of the devil's ploy to do away with the Son of God.

Who, then, sent the "star"? Well, who had the greatest interest in seeing the child Jesus put to death, preventing him from growing up and fulfilling his mission on earth? Who seeks to mislead people and promotes lies, violence, and slaughter? Jesus himself identified the "liar and the father of the lie," the one who "was a manslayer when he began"—Satan the Devil (Watch Tower, 2017).

REDEEMED ASTROLOGERS

In the Bible, it is stated that the Wise Men were meaning to find Jesus not to cause Him harm, but rather to "come to worship Him" (Matthew 2:2). Though the star was discovered and followed by these astrologers, it was meant to be a sign of hope to foreign people, the Gentiles, as well as to those most in need of redemption. Saints John Chrysostom and Augustine, both Doctors of the Church, believed that the star was a means by God to purposely attract the Gentiles of the East, that Christ chose to make Himself known not to just the Jews but also to the Gentiles of Persia.

> God calls them by means of the things they are most familiar with; and He shows them a large and extraordinary star so that they would be impressed by its size and beauty (University of Navarre, 2005, pg. 30).

> The shepherds were Israelites, the Magi were Gentiles. The former were nigh to Him, the latter far from Him. Both hastened to Him together as to the cornerstone ... As unskillfulness predominates in the rustic manners of the shepherds, so ungodliness abounds in the profane rites of the Magi. Yet did this

Corner-Stone draw both to itself; inasmuch as He came 'to choose the foolish things that He might confound the wise', and 'not to call the just, but sinners' (T. Aquinas, 2014).

The Bible says that when the Magi found where Jesus was, they "rejoiced exceedingly" and "falling down, they worshipped Him (Matthew 2:11)." The Magi are described as falling down and this is important to note that in the Jewish traditions kneeling or prostration before someone was seen as undignified. To this day, people of the Jewish faith do not kneel when they pray, but rather they stand. This was the complete opposite for the Persians; to them kneeling was a sign of the greatest reverence and used when venerating a recognized King. To this day kneeling is an important element of Christian worship, particularly within the Catholic Church where in addition to kneeling, genuflecting is also a part of worship. Eastern tradition holds that after they adored the Infant Jesus and presented their gifts the Virgin Mary gave them, as a token of friendship, some of our Lord's garments to bring back with them to the East. The Magi returned to Persia and in the year 40 A.D. they were baptized by St. Thomas the Apostle. Later killed for their faith in Christ, Gaspar, Melchior, and Balthasar were celebrated as martyrs and saints. In renaissance art, they are often depicted with halos.

JOSEPH'S ANGEL ANNOUNCES THE WISE MEN TO HIM

Mother Cecelia Baij reveals that St. Joseph prayed for people to learn of the gift God had given them in the person of His Son. He wanted to share this with the whole world. The Lord answered Joseph with another visitation of one of Joseph's angels:

The joyous Joseph wished for the world to know of this great favour that God had given to mankind in sending His Only Begotten Son for its salvation. ... Joseph's angel then came to reveal to him that three kings from the East were coming to adore the newly-born Saviour ... Joseph was told that he had every reason to rejoice over this since it would satisfy the desires of his heart and would be an answer to his petitions that Jesus be known (C. Baij, 1997, pg. 165).

ST. JOSEPH'S COURT

Some have wondered what the purpose was of the Magi meeting in Herod's palace before finding the Holy Family. St. John Chrysostom speaks:

> The star had been hidden from them so that, on finding themselves without their guide, they would have no alternative but to consult the Jews (in King Herod's court.) In this way, the birth of Jesus would be made known to all (University of Navarre, 2005, pg. 30).

After leaving the extravagant court of King Herod, the three Wise Men found themselves in the humble court of St. Joseph. He felt especially honoured to receive these esteemed men as guests and respectfully invited them in to adore the Infant Jesus. These men, who were used to the finer things in life, gladly set aside their pomp for the humble surroundings they now found themselves in. After adoring the Holy Child, Blessed Anne Catherine Emmerich reveals that St. Joseph was a most gracious host:

> Meanwhile Joseph ... had set out a light meal in the kings' tent ... I saw Joseph receiving them with great friendliness and begging them to be his guests and accept this modest meal. He reclined among them

around the low table as they ate. He was not at all shy, and was so happy (A. Emmerich, 1953, pg. 161).

At this gathering there were no rich or poor, royal or lowly, but rather they were all men of equal standing. Though the Magi had come to see the new born King of the Jews expecting to be led to a palace, they knew that upon entering the humble Nativity cave they were in fact in the royal court of a king whose kingdom was not of this world (John 18:36).

The throne Christ sat upon was not of gold or set with diamonds, but rather was the lap of the Blessed Virgin Mary – the jewel of God's creation. The Divine Infant King was not clothed in robes of fine silks, but in simple swaddling clothes and Joseph's cloak. St. Joseph, though not outwardly of royal nobility since his family no longer sat on the throne of David, was the Prince of this little kingdom on earth and was the most gracious and noble of those men present.

> When God the Father decided to give His Son to the world, He wanted to do so with honour, since He is worthy of all honour and glory. He thus prepared Him a court and royal service worthy of Him: God desired that His Son should have an honourable and glorious reception on earth, if not in the eyes of the world, at least in His own eyes ... The court of the Son of God made Man was composed of Mary and Joseph: God Himself could not have found more worthy servants for His Son (P. Eymard, 2008).

CHAPTER 6: THE PRESENTATION

This chapter speaks of the Presentation of Jesus in the Temple forty days after His birth.

> I delight to do Your will, O my God; Your Law is within my heart (Psalm 40:8-10 NASB).

Forty days after the birth of Jesus, it was time for Joseph to take his wife and son to the Temple at Jerusalem. The Law stated that after the birth of a child, the mother had to wait 33 days to purified and, though Mary herself was Immaculate, she willed to submit herself to the rite of Purification, just as her son was subjected to the circumcision. The Presentation was a ceremony in which the father would present his first-born son to be redeemed under God. The child would be "ransomed", bought back from God with an offering, and Joseph and Mary followed the Law as it was prescribed.

> And when the days for their purification according to the law of Moses were completed, they brought Him up to Jerusalem to present Him to the Lord (Luke 2:22 NASB).

SIMEON

St. Joseph brought his family to the Jerusalem Temple to present his son, not knowing what else was in store. At the Temple was Simeon, a devout priest of Jerusalem who, according to the Gospel of St. Luke, was awaiting the coming of the Messiah with great anticipation. The Bible says that he was quite old and wished desperately to see the "consolation of Israel" (St. Luke 2:25) before he died. His prayers were answered when he was given a revelation from the Holy Spirit stating that the time would come for him to behold the Promised One. Simeon was the first man at the Temple to recognize and revere the Saviour and hold the Child Jesus in his venerable arms, praising and thanking God for granting him this honour:

> "Now thou dost dismiss Thy servant, O Lord, according to Thy word, in peace; because my eyes have seen Thy salvation, which Thou hast prepared before the face of all peoples: a light of revelation to the Gentiles, and a glory for Thy people Israel (Luke 2:29-32 DRV).

HEARTS OF SORROW INTERTWINED

After hearing this Canticle of Simeon, and marveling at his words, Joseph and Mary were then given a prophecy by the venerable priest concerning their son, as well as words concerning the very soul of the Blessed Virgin Mary:

> And Simeon blessed them, and said to Mary his mother: Behold this child is set for the fall, and for the resurrection of many in Israel, and for a sign which shall be contradicted; And thy own soul a sword shall pierce, that, out of many hearts, thoughts may be revealed (Luke 2:34-36 DRV).

Mother Cecelia Baij reveals Joseph's sorrow at hearing the words of Simeon:

> Joseph was afflicted with sorrow when the prophet said this because he was, to a certain extent, aware what these words implied. He tried to subdue his feelings of anguish, but he succumbed and wept bitterly. The words of Simeon were now imprinted upon his heart and they caused him constant affliction (C. Baij, 1997, pg. 175).

The most humble heart of Joseph would be in full union with that of his spouse, which together would carry a unique agony known only to them. Besides sharing this with Mary, St. Joseph had his own private affliction of knowing that he would not be there to protect his suffering boy or comfort his spouse when the time of the falling, rising, and contradiction centered around Jesus, and pierced soul of Mary, would come to fulfill the words of Simeon. Since he was not mentioned in Simeon's prophecies, he knew that he might not live to witness these events. He knew that he would not be there to shield and protect those whom the Lord had lovingly entrusted to him. These hearts of Joseph and Mary brought together by the Will of the God, in love, were now intertwined in sorrow, each one to be the consolation of the other.

> The holy spouse St. Joseph was, by these prophecies, made to see many of the mysteries of the Redemption and of the labours and sufferings of Jesus. ... However, Saint Joseph was not to be an eyewitness of them during his mortal life (M. Agreda, 1912, p. 511).

PROPHETESS ANNA

After contemplating these things, the priest Simeon blessed and prayed over Mary, giving St. Joseph a special blessing as well. After these words, God sent to Joseph and Mary a consolation by means of Anna the prophetess who bore public witness to the greatness of God. It is traditionally held that Anna knew the Blessed Virgin when she was a child, teaching her in the ways of the Lord.

> And there was one Anna, a prophetess ... Now she, at the same hour, coming in, confessed to the Lord;

and spoke of Him to all that looked for the redemption of Israel (Luke 2:36-38 DRV).

JOSEPH PRESENTS HIS SON

Joseph fulfills the Law's requirement to present his son to God to be redeemed by a sacrifice of two turtledoves. St. Joseph had just fulfilled his second official act as father to Jesus, having presented and consecrated Him at the Temple of Jerusalem. Just as with the circumcision of Jesus, the Law required that the first-born son be redeemed. Joseph brought Jesus into the Inner Court of the Temple, in which women were not allowed, the Blessed Virgin waiting outside. He carried into the Temple the True High Priest though no one would recognize the child as such nor would they pay him homage. In the midst of the Temple was the Messiah Himself — the one's arrival the Jews were earnestly praying for, though it was only the venerable Simeon and Anna who saw the Redeemer in this child. Jesus was to become the Sacrificial Lamb who, years later, would carry the cross upon which He would die for the redemption of the world. At the Presentation, His burden is not yet apparent as He is carried into the Temple by His most faithful servant, Joseph, who "buys back" the Infant Jesus from God the Father. Pope Francis speaks on the importance of this event:

> Before our eyes is a humble but great event: Mary and Joseph take Jesus to the Temple of Jerusalem. He is a baby as so many others, but He is unique: He is the Only-Begotten come for all. ... In the Temple Jesus comes to meet us ... We contemplate the meeting with the elderly Simeon, who represents the faithful expectation of Israel and the exultation of the heart for the fulfillment of the ancient promises. We

also admire the meeting with the elderly prophetess Anna, who, on seeing the Child, praises God. Simeon and Anna are the expectation and the prophecy; Jesus is the novelty and the fulfillment: He presents Himself to us as the endless surprise of God. In this Child, born for all, the past — made of memory and promise –, and the future — full of hope, come together (Francis, 2016).

CHAPTER 7: THE CHILD HUNTED

This chapter speaks of the abuses suffered by Joseph in Nazareth, the messenger angel returning to him, King Herod's massacre of the innocents, and Joseph leading his family in exile to Egypt

After St. Joseph had fulfilled his duty of presenting Jesus, and the Blessed Virgin receiving her purification in the eyes of the Law, the Holy Family turned their thoughts towards settling down and making a home for themselves. It was Joseph's hope that they would reside in Nazareth and live a peaceful life. However, upon arriving, Joseph was met with abuses from the townspeople who labeled him a brute for taking the Virgin Mary on the rough journey to Bethlehem, knowing how close she was to giving birth. The return to Nazareth was not as peaceful as Joseph had hoped as he was vilified by the townspeople - some of whom were influenced by the devil. St. Joseph was no stranger to the devil nor to the insults of man, as he had experienced this to some extent in his childhood, as recorded earlier in this book. Just as he endured these abuses as a child, with holy patience, so did he in his adulthood, though with great suffering. Mother Cecelia Baij reveals:

> ... they began to abuse him and declared him a brute for having taken his spouse to Bethlehem at a time when her delivery was imminent. Some had been stirred up by the devil to attack Joseph further by proclaiming that it was a folly to have given the maiden Mary as spouse to a man like him, that he had no concern for her, and allowed her to suffer. They declared that he would be to blame if she suffered a premature death from the sufferings he caused her. These abuses were as so many swords piercing the heart of the loving Joseph, for he knew how much he

loved his spouse, and how grateful he had been to God for having given her to him (C. Baij, 1997, pg. 181).

Though saddened and wounded by these abuses, St. Joseph continued to excel in his virtues of patience, humility, and love for all. He was always pleasing in the sight of God, his spouse Mary, and the Divine Infant Jesus. Mother Cecelia Baij reveals the beautiful words of adoration that Joseph spoke amid his trials, and the ecstasy he experienced as reward for his love:

> "Oh my God, ... How is it possible that You, Who are Infinite Goodness, Perfection, and Unfathomable Beauty, are not loved by all men?" With these words Joseph went into an ecstasy for several hours, delighting in the grandeur of God. He became as on fire with most holy love for God. ... After the ecstasy, Mary placed the Divine Infant in Joseph's arms. Joseph pressed Him to his bosom and thereby provided full satisfaction to his love-hungry heart. His soul was refreshed by this embrace with his beloved God (C. Baij, 1997, pg. 181, 182).

THE PLOT AGAINST THE CHILD JESUS

Being the head of the Holy Family and its appointed guide and provider, Joseph received a startling message from one of his angels:

> "Arise, and take the Child and His mother, and fly into Egypt: and be there until I shall tell thee. For it will come to pass that Herod will seek the Child to destroy Him (Matthew 2:13 DRV)."

In the Gospel of St. Matthew, it is implied that the Holy Family was still in Bethlehem when St. Joseph received this message from the angel. However, Blessed Ann Catherine Emmerich and Mother Cecelia Baij claim it was revealed to them that Joseph had already settled his family seventy miles north of Bethlehem, at Nazareth:

> In Nazareth ... I saw Joseph in his room lying on his side asleep with his head on his arm. I saw a shining youth come up to his bed and speak with him. The youth took his hand and pulled him up, when Joseph came to his senses and got up, on which the youth disappeared (A. Emmerich, 1953, pg.183).

> ... Joseph felt quite content to remain in Nazareth, but when he heard of Herod's persecution he was stricken with deepest anguish (C. Baij, 1997, pg. 182).

Joseph woke Mary straight away and they left in haste. The words of Simeon, the elder from the Temple, echoed in their minds: "Behold, this child is destined for the fall and rise of many!" (St. Luke 2:34) Could this already be the beginning fulfillment of his words? Jesus was barely two months old and already He had stirred up hope in the lowly and fear in the mighty! To St. Joseph was given the responsibility of safeguarding the lives of the Christ Child, as well as that of the Blessed Virgin. The Wise Men of the East had inquired to Herod about the birth of the King of the Jews in Bethlehem and this made him nervous. Rather than risk losing his crown, Herod acted on his insecurities and anger by sending his soldiers throughout the land of Judea to kill every boy under the age of two years. While soldiers went about tearing infants away from their mothers' breasts, and toddlers from their father's arms, the Holy Family was already far into the desert.

When Herod realized that he had been outwitted by the Magi, he was furious, and he gave orders to kill all the boys in Bethlehem and its vicinity who were two years old and under (Matthew 2:16 NIV).

Thus, says the Lord, "A voice is heard in Ramah, lamentation and bitter weeping. Rachel is weeping for her children; She refuses to be comforted for her children, because they are no more (Jeremiah 31:15 NASB)."

ST. JOSEPH, A MAN OF ACTION

The angel had given no other instruction than to flee to Egypt and to remain there until further word. This uncertainty would have been incredibly distressful to Joseph, but he being a perfect model of obedience to the Will of God asked no questions and acted straight away. He stands in great contrast to the great Lawgiver Moses who made numerous inquiries and hesitations as the Lord commanded him to bring the Israelites out of Egypt, even though the Lord had promised to be among him and his people. The Lord even said that He would show many signs and wonders for their consolation, and yet they complained and caused themselves grief.

Joseph was commanded by the angel to get up and go; no help was promised, no directions given, and no words of consolation. In the Gospel of St. Matthew, Joseph is shown to be a man of faith and a man of action — obedient upon receiving his instructions, and a perfect example of complete submission to the Divine Will. Joseph, having had no certainty of what would come next for his family, led them into to Egypt as fugitives. Though anxiety weighed on the young father and husband, he was determined to carry out the angel's instructions; he continued to place his filial trust in God, as mentioned by Mother Cecelia Baij:

Who arose, and took the child and His mother by night, and retired into Egypt (Matthew 2:14 DRV).

Joseph's angel spoke to him, commanding him to take the Child and His mother into Egypt. The angel made it clear that Herod was passionately determined that the Child be killed. ... Being real fugitives, they stole away at night. Joseph did not know exactly what course to take to get to Egypt, so he abandoned himself entirely to Divine Providence (C. Baij, 1997, pg. 183, 184).

Concerning this man of action, Pope Benedict XVI contemplates the faith and fidelity of St. Joseph:

In Joseph, faith is not separated from action. His faith had a decisive effect on his actions. Paradoxically, it was by acting, by carrying out his responsibilities, that he stepped aside and left God free to act, placing no obstacles in His way. Joseph is a 'just' man because his existence is 'ad-justed' to the word of God (Benedict XVI, 2009).

The sun beginning to rise, and cover of darkness slowly vanishing, the Blessed Virgin prayed silently over her boy, her lips whispered a prayer for divine help in her hour of need and especially for Joseph, her just husband, who was leading them into exile:

Hearken to the voice of my prayer, O my King and my God ... In the morning I will stand before Thee ...

> Conduct me, O Lord, in Thy justice: because of my
> enemies, direct my way in Thy sight ... For Thou wilt
> bless the just. O Lord, Thou hast crowned us, as with
> a shield of Thy good will (Psalm 5:3-5, 9, 13 DRV).

Though his wife prayed quietly, Joseph heard her pleas to the Lord and was touched. She was a strong woman and though she cried, her tears filled him with the strength to walk onward, regardless of how tired his feet were.

> "Restrain your voice from weeping, and your eyes
> from tears; for your sorrow will be rewarded,"
> declares the Lord (Jeremiah 31:16 NASB).

Christ was Joseph's love and salvation and though He was not of his flesh, Jesus was still his son. And if he kept his faith in the Lord — especially during trials and sufferings — Joseph would not fail in his service to Him. As the terrain turned rougher, the Holy Family spent several days walking in the hot sun and sleeping under whatever shelter they could find. Also, Joseph got very little sleep since he kept watch almost all night, as it was not uncommon to hear stories of travelers being robbed and even killed in the desert!

There is a tradition as early as the 3rd century, found predominantly in the Eastern Church, that the Holy Family encountered thieves in the desert. Upon traveling, St. Joseph and his family found themselves in an area inhabited by a band of thieves – one of whom was named Dismas. Dismas saw this vulnerable family approaching and was about to attack and rob them when his eyes saw the face of the Divine Infant. It is said that he recognized the Child Jesus as his Lord and at once repented. In one of his sermons Blessed James of Voragine speaks of this encounter:

During their flight into Egypt the Holy Family fell into the hands of robbers. One of them, ravished by the beauty of the Child, said to his companions: 'Verily I say to you that if it were possible for God to assume our nature, I should believe this Child to be God.' ... they allowed the Holy Family to depart unhurt (M. Lisle, 1882, pg. 18).

It is said that later at the crucifixion of Jesus, Dismas was the thief to the right hand of our Lord, in whom he professed his faith, and asked pardon. Traditionally on a crucifix, Jesus tilts His head to His right-hand side, acknowledging the reverence paid to Him by the Good Thief.

And he said to Jesus: Lord, remember me when thou shalt come into Thy kingdom (Luke 23:42 DRV).

THE HOLY INNOCENTS

Meanwhile, Herod's fury raged in Bethlehem and its surrounding towns, innocent blood streamed down the streets as mothers and fathers wept for their sons. Had the angel not warned St. Joseph, it would have been him fighting to save his only son. It would have been his wife, sobbing in the streets. It would have been his boy who was killed by the sword of an insecure king. These sons were the first martyrs to spill their blood for Jesus Christ — these Holy Innocents died for Christ without even knowing, but great is their reward in Heaven.

After construction of the Church of the Nativity, built over the spot of Christ's birth, the Empress St. Helena brought the relics of some of these little children and placed them in one of the church's underground chapels, which was subsequently dedicated to their memory. Under the altar reposed the little bones of these innocent children, beloved by God and His Church. The Roman Catholic Church celebrates these victim children, piously referred to as the "Holy Innocents", on December 28th. The Church also names them, in the words of St. Augustine, the "Flowers of the Martyrs" as they were the buds of the new Church, being cut down in the persecution of Herod.

> ... I saw under the altar the souls of them that were slain for the word of God (Apocalypse 6:9 DRV).

> The Church venerates these children as martyrs (flores martyrum); they are the first buds of the Church killed by the frost of persecution; they died not only for Christ, but in His stead (K. Knight, 2017).

Joseph's important role in safely conducting the Son of God and His mother in exile is often overlooked, however Pope Leo XIII acknowledged this great feat in his encyclical, *Quamquam Pluries*:

> Joseph guarded from death the Child threatened by a monarch's jealousy, and found for Him a refuge; in the miseries of the journey and in the bitterness of exile he was ever the companion, the assistance, and the upholder of the Virgin and of Jesus (Leo XIII, 1889).

CHAPTER 8: REFUGEES

This chapter speaks of the journey to Egypt, the toppling of the idols, life in Egypt, and healings.

> How much St. Joseph must have suffered on the journey into Egypt in seeing the sufferings of Jesus and Mary! ... Joseph was indeed conformed in all things to the will of the Eternal Father, but his tender and loving heart could not but feel pain in seeing the Son of God trembling and weeping from cold and the other hardships which he experienced on that hard journey (A. Liguori, 2017).

After many days of hazardous travel, Joseph and his family would finally cross into Egypt, a sigh of relief granted. They were now safe, but as they made their way through Egypt, they received many strange looks from people, as they were foreigners and were not to be trusted.

Everything had happened so quickly since Joseph married his beloved: firstly, he had the dilemma of his virgin bride being found pregnant with the Son of God. At that time his heart was full of fear and anxiety until the angel appeared to him and reassured him. Secondly, once he and Mary were together as husband and wife, he had to travel to Bethlehem for the census. This journey was difficult for him, especially since his wife was close to giving birth and they had yet to find lodgings. Being everywhere refused he found shelter in a cave where Mary had given birth to our Lord. He guarded his wife and child, aware that thieves or other criminals might seek to hide there or worse, to rob them of the few possessions they had. Thirdly, Joseph had been warned of King Herod's intention to have the child executed, and he then had to flee with Mary and Jesus in the middle of the night and travel to a foreign land.

He saw the children of Bethlehem in his mind and he wept for them in his heart. He wept for his wife, whose soul was being pierced at the thought of all those innocents being taken away from their mothers. He wept for his Son, who was being persecuted by a man who was known to have had one of his wives, three of his sons, and his brother-in-law executed for suspected treason. The steps to Egypt were stained with the tears of Joseph and Mary as they travelled the rough terrain under the hot sun and cold night sky. The child Jesus was carried into a foreign land as a fugitive, though He had committed no crime.

THE IDOLS TOPPLE

They finally arrived in Egypt, the land of strange gods, not as visitors but as refugees fleeing their own country. Servant of God Mother Cecilia Baij reveals that Joseph feared the reception that his family might receive among the pagans of this place and, being of a self-sacrificial nature, as every father should be, pleaded for God to spare his spouse and Son any mistreatment during their sojourn and to let it fall upon him in their place:

> At length, after having endured many trials, Jesus, Mary and Joseph reached their destination in Egypt. Joseph dreaded this entry, fearing these people, being barbarous and idolatrous, would mistreat them. He, therefore, turned to God in fervent supplication, saying:

> "Oh my God, grant me the favour that your Only-Begotten Son, and His holy mother, may never be subjected to such outrages. Look down upon me, as I offer to take everything upon myself. If only they be spared from such adversities. My God do not permit that they, who are so innocent, so exceedingly

110

virtuous, so rich in merit, shall be mistreated. I deserve every misfortune. Permit, therefore, that these things happen only to me, and not to them (C. Baij, 1997, pg. 191).

Little did the Egyptians know that Joseph and Mary carried the One True God and brought Him into their midst. Upon the entry of the Christ Child, the many idols of Egypt trembled and fell causing a panic and sadness among the people, in fulfillment of the prophecy of Isaiah, and confirmed by the mystics Mother Cecilia Baij and Venerable Maria de Agreda:

> Behold, the Lord is riding ... to Egypt; the idols of Egypt will tremble at His presence, and the heart of the Egyptians will melt within them (Isaiah 19:1 NASB).

> As they made their entry, the idols to which these blinded people rendered their adoration fell toppling to the ground. This caused a considerable stir among the inhabitants, since no one had any idea what could be bringing this about. How could they know that it was the true God Himself who was thus destroying their false gods as He entered their city (C. Baij, 1997, pg. 192).

> On entering the towns of Egypt, the divine Infant, in the arms of His mother, raised His eyes and His hands to the Father asking for the salvation of these inhabitants held captive by Satan. And immediately He made use of His sovereign and divine power and drove the demons from the idols and hurled them to the infernal abyss. Like lightning flashing from the clouds, they darted forth and descended to the lowermost caverns of Hell and darkness. At the same

instant, the idols crashed to the ground, the altars fell to pieces, and the temples crumbled to ruins. St. Joseph knew this to be the work of the incarnate Word; and he praised and extolled Him in holy admiration. The Egyptian people were astounded at these inexplicable happenings (M. Agreda, 1912, p. 551).

STOPS OF THE HOLY FAMILY

It is believed that the Holy Family did not just settle at the first town or city they encountered in Egypt but were constantly on the move to find a suitable place of safety. The angel did not tell Joseph how long they would have to stay in exile, so until hearing again from the messenger, they would travel throughout Egypt. Tradition states that they stayed in Egypt for seven years before returning to their homeland and settling in Nazareth.

Per Eastern tradition, Theophilus (Coptic Patriarch of Alexandria from A.D. 385-412) had a vision in which he was shown the Holy Family's escape route and the many places in Egypt at which they rested. He states that Joseph and his family fled to Gaza and then to El-Zaraniq, which is about thirty-eight kilometers west of El-Arish. After weeks of further travel, the Holy Family made plenty of rest stops, among them was Matariyah where a miracle was performed by the Divine Infant:

> In Matareyah, a tree still stands to this day, still regularly visited, called Mary's Tree, for the Family is believed to have rested in its shade. Here, too, the Infant Jesus caused water to flow from a spring, from which He drank and blessed, and in which the Virgin washed His clothes. She poured the washing water on to the ground, and from that spot, the fragrant

balsam plant blossomed: besides the healing and pain-soothing properties of this balm, its essence is used in the preparation of the scents and perfumes of which the holy Chrism (oil) is composed (State Information Service of Egypt, 2017).

This next tradition has been immortalized in works of art over the centuries: Mary is exhausted and wishes to rest a while in the shade of a tree. She does not want to trouble Joseph, and yet he does not seek rest until she recommends it. He is totally devoted to his spouse's comfort and well-being. When the Virgin Mary mentions that she is tired and would like to rest, Joseph pauses their journey and leads the family to the shade of a tree. Mary tells him that she is hungry and would like some fruit:

> And it came to pass... while they were walking, that the blessed Mary was fatigued ... and seeing a palm tree, she said to Joseph: Let me rest a little under the shade of this tree. Joseph therefore made haste, and led her to the palm ... And blessed Mary was sitting there, she looked up ... and saw it full of fruit and said to Joseph: I wish it were possible to get some of the fruit of this palm. And Joseph said to her: I wonder that you say this, when you see how high the palm tree is; and that you think of eating of its fruit. I am thinking more of the want of water, because the skins are now empty, and we have none wherewith to refresh ourselves and our cattle. Then the child Jesus, with a joyful countenance ... said to the palm: O tree, bend your branches, and refresh my mother with your fruit. And immediately at these words the palm bent its top down to the very feet of the blessed Mary; and they gathered its fruit, with which they were all refreshed. ... Then Jesus said to it: ... open

113

from your roots a vein of water which has been hid in the earth, and let the waters flow, so that we may be satisfied from you ... and at its root there began to come forth a spring of water exceedingly clear and cool and sparkling. And when they saw the spring of water, they rejoiced (K. Knight, 2017).

ALTAR TO THE LORD

St. Joseph led his family to Mount Qussqam, which would be the most important and most meaningful stop for them in the land of Egypt as it fulfilled yet another prophecy from the Prophet Isaiah:

> ... there will be an altar to the Lord in the midst of the land of Egypt, and a pillar to the Lord near its border. It will become a sign and a witness to the Lord of hosts in the land of Egypt; ... Thus, the Lord will make Himself known to Egypt (Isaiah 19:19-21, NASB).

At this place there now stands the Al-Muharraq Monastery, within it the Church of the Virgin Mary, the altar-stone once being the bed upon which the young Jesus slept. This altar-stone is believed to be the fulfillment of part of the Isaiah prophecy. As for the mentioned pillar, it is held to be the Patriarchal See of the Apostolic Church in Egypt, believed to have been established by St. Mark in Alexandria — on Egypt's Northern border.

LIFE IN EGYPT

While in exile St. Joseph was troubled by the idolatry of the Egyptians and he pitied these people. Joseph began his intercessory role in the land of pagans by praying for their conversion while also doing good deeds for them regardless of their beliefs. Though the exile from his native land would be hard for Joseph, he always had the consolation of his blessed spouse Mary and the Divine Child Jesus. Mother Cecelia Baij recounts:

> Joseph was always very much concerned for the conversion of all sinners and would plead with God on their behalf whenever he found such souls ... Living as he did among these unbelievers, he therefore, strove all the more to demonstrate his love for his fellow-man ... and, poor as he was, he still bestowed alms ... Though he worked diligently, Joseph never failed in his prayers. ... Sometimes he was tired from his strenuous labours, and when he came back to Mary, he would tell her of it. She would place the Infant Jesus in his arms ... The happy Joseph would receive Him in deepest humility and embracing Him ... his soul would be filled with joy and consolation (C. Baij, 1997, pg. 195, 199).

Besides working amongst the pagans to provide for the Blessed Virgin Mary and the Child Jesus, St. Joseph also sought out fellow Jews who were living and working in Egypt. Blessed Anne Catherine Emmerich reveals that Joseph not only befriended his fellow-Jews, but he built for them a small house of prayer. During their stay in Egypt the Child Jesus, who grew considerably, would often accompany Joseph on his errands and his work:

> Joseph built a place of prayer in which the Jews living in the city assembled together with the Holy Family. Before this they had no meeting-place for prayer. I was often shown how the little Jesus was already growing bigger, and how He played with other children. He could already speak and run quite well;

He was often with Joseph, and sometimes went with him when he worked away from home (A. Emmerich, 1953, pg.193).

THE POWER TO HEAL

While in Egypt, it is said that during their seven years there, the Blessed Virgin Mary and her spouse St. Joseph would preach to the Egyptians and even perform healings in the name of their Son. Venerable Maria de Agreda reveals:

> Many books would be required to describe the wonders and the conversions of souls that took place during the seven years of their stay in Egypt. ... Whenever Mary listened to and answered those that came to her, she held in her arms the Infant Jesus, as the One who was the Author of all the graces to be dispensed to sinners. The Child Jesus empowered her to cure women with the touch of her hands.
>
> ... While living in Heliopolis there was a period of pestilence. People knew of the healings that had taken place and came to them from all parts of the country and returned home cured in body and soul. St. Joseph, too, was ordained by God in the teaching and healing of the infirm. For this purpose, he was endowed with new light and the power of healing. He ordinarily taught and cured the men, while the blessed Lady attended to the women. (M. Agreda, 1912, p. 569, 572).

THE MESSENGER RETURNS

It was reportedly at Al-Muharraq that the messenger angel came once again to instruct the Lord's most humble servant. St. Joseph had been waiting for this moment for quite some time and finally it came to him as revealed in the Gospel of St. Matthew:

> ... an angel of the Lord appeared in a dream to Joseph in Egypt, and said, "Get up, take the Child and His mother, and go into the land of Israel; for those who sought the Child's life are dead." So, Joseph got up, took the Child and His mother, and came into the land of Israel. (Matthew 2:19-21 NASB).

Joseph's paternal heart was overjoyed that he could now bring his son and wife home. However, Herod's son Archelaus had ascended the throne and was reputed to also be a tyrant. It is said that Joseph was afraid to return to Judea, with the angel appearing to him once more to redirect him to Galilee:

> But when he heard that Archelaus was reigning over Judea in place of his father Herod, he was afraid to go there. Then after being warned by God in a dream, he left for the regions of Galilee, and came and lived in a city called Nazareth (Matthew 2:22-23 NASB).

This passage from Matthew is often passed over quickly without a word or thought, but even this brief scene merits mention. In it is found that St. Joseph is afraid to return to Judea with his family, fearing that Herod's successor would seek to destroy his son. Though he has faith, Joseph still has a temporal fear which is a part of the human condition, and the Heavenly Father understands this. So once again the Lord sends His messenger to instruct Joseph on what he is to do. This mention of Joseph's fear speaks volumes not only about human frailties but also of God's compassion. The Heavenly Father allows Joseph to have, to a certain extent, self-reliance — even if it allows for him to fear. But the Lord is merciful, and so He sends His messenger to advise Joseph on the course he should take to bring his family safely out of exile.

The entire journey to Al-Muharraq and back to Nazareth had covered over two thousand kilometers. Joseph, who would have led his family in and out of exile by foot, would have taken each step for the greater glory of God. Though the years of exile were built on the foundation of sadness, the return home was built on joy. His faith continued to guide him forward.

> Let your eyes look directly forward, and your gaze be straight before you. Take heed to the path of your feet, then all your ways will be sure. Do not swerve to the right or to the left; turn your foot away from evil (Proverbs 4:25-27 RSVCE).

> And so, Jesus' way back to Nazareth from Bethlehem passed through Egypt. Just as Israel had followed the path of the exodus "from the condition of slavery" in order to begin the Old Covenant, so Joseph, guardian and cooperator in the providential mystery of God, even in exile watched over the one who brings about the New Covenant (John Paul II, 1989).

CHAPTER 9: SON OF JOSEPH

This chapter speaks of the return to Nazareth, St. Joseph's relationship with his Divine Son Jesus, and the loss and finding of Jesus in Jerusalem.

And they said: Is not this Jesus, the son of Joseph, whose father and mother we know (John 6:42 DRV)?

There is but one fatherhood, that of God the Father, the one Creator of the world, of all that is seen and unseen. Yet man, created in the image of God, has been granted a share in this one paternity of God (Ephesians 3:15). Saint Joseph is a striking case of this, since he is a father, without fatherhood according to the flesh. He is not the biological father of Jesus, whose Father is God alone, and yet he lives his fatherhood fully and completely. To be a father means above all to be at the service of life and growth. Saint Joseph, in this sense, gave proof of great devotion. For the sake of Christ, he experienced persecution, exile and the poverty which this entails. He had to settle far from his native town. His only reward was to be with Christ. His readiness to do all these things illustrates the words of Saint Paul: "It is Christ the Lord whom you serve (Colossians 3:24)." (Benedict XVI, 2009).

The Holy Bible does not give us a full account of the life of the Holy Family except for a brief mention in the Gospel of St. Luke, when Jesus is already twelve years of age. These hidden years were filled with everyday joys and sorrows, as with other families. Per Venerable Maria de Agreda, upon arriving at their home in Nazareth, St. Joseph straightaway set out to re-establish himself as a carpenter, opening his shop to earn a living for his family. She contrasts the labours of St. Joseph to other "sons of Adam":

> Holy Joseph ordered his occupations and his work to most worthily provide for the divine Child and His mother, as well as for himself. That, which in other sons of Adam is considered a punishment and a hardship, was to this holy Patriarch a great happiness. For while others were condemned to sustain their natural life by the labour of their hands in the sweat of their brows, Saint Joseph was blessed and consoled beyond measure to know, that he had been chosen by his labour and sweat to support God Himself and His mother (M. Agreda, 1912, p. 606).

THE CLOSENESS OF JESUS AND JOSEPH

As years went by, Joseph, having established his family and his work in Nazareth, went on to teach his Son in the ways of life. There is no doubt that he could learn and gain various illuminations from his Son, the Son of God. But it happened that Jesus chose to respect and recognize Joseph's intelligence, his hard work and his human nature. In renaissance art, Joseph is sometimes depicted as being in the background, not playing an active part in the life of Christ, when the exact opposite is true. St. Joseph, the Virgin-Father of Jesus, spent the most amount of time with Him, besides His Blessed Mother. St. Joseph was Jesus' model of manhood and taught Him, who is both God and Man, what it is to be a mortal man. Saints Ephrem and Peter Julian Eymard praise the paternity of Joseph:

> Blessed are you, O just Joseph, for He who became a child grew up at your side taking you for His model; The Word lived under your roof, though never

leaving the Father. Blessed are the names He has taken in His love: He who was the Son of the Father is called son of David, son of Joseph (L. Cristiani, 1967, pg. 89-90).

When Joseph embraced Jesus in his arms, acts of loving faith welled up constantly in his heart. It was a worship that pleased our Lord more than that which He receives in Heaven. Picture, for yourself, Saint Joseph adoring his Son as His God. He tells of his readiness to die for Christ, of all his plans to promote Christ's glory, and to win more souls to His love. No lover builds more scintillating plans for his loved one than a saint. The purer and simpler a soul, the more magnificent it's love and adoration. No matter what you do, your adoration will never equal in worth that of St. Joseph. Join with his merits. A soul that loves God offers everything to Him in love and God listens to such a soul, which is worth a thousand others (P. Eymard, 2017).

FATHER AND TEACHER

If princes of this world are most careful in choosing tutors for their sons, taking pains to secure the best that can be found, do you think that God did not select the man who was the most perfectly qualified to be the guardian of His Eternal Son, the Lord of Heaven and earth (F.Sales, 2017).

St. Joseph taught the Word, Jesus, how to read, how to pray, and how to work just like any other father would teach his son. The scholastic view of Joseph as teacher is rarely thought of among the theologians or painted in the arts. However, during the seventeenth century, many artists began to portray him as somewhat of a scholar, with an open book in front of him. In some of these paintings, he is pointing to a verse in the book, which is assumed to be the Scriptures, as he gazes lovingly at the Child Jesus. Joseph was aware of the prophecies that spoke of a future Messiah, and the depiction of him with the book, while looking at Jesus, is revealing that Jesus will fulfill the words of the prophets. Let it not be assumed that because he worked with his hands, Joseph was illiterate and did not read the words of the prophets. As was shown in Chapter Two of Part One, Joseph was taught by his own father, Jacob, in his childhood.

It is said in Scripture that when Jesus came to this earth, He emptied Himself and did not cling to His divinity, to be like one of us (Philippians 2:5-9). Jesus genuinely willed Himself to learn from His virgin-father on earth and to grow as any other boy would. Joseph was a father, guardian, and teacher to his son. This Joseph is both worker and intellectual, and he passed these ideals on to Christ.

Pope Francis reflects on the various aspects of the fatherhood of St. Joseph:

> We look at Joseph – as the model of the educator, who safeguards and accompanies Jesus in His journey of growth in "wisdom, years and grace", as the Gospel of Luke tells us ... Joseph took care of Jesus, ... he raised Him, ensuring His healthy development.
>
> In Nazareth, there is the hidden life of Jesus within the Holy Family. During those years, Joseph taught Jesus his work, Jesus learned to be a carpenter. Joseph was an example and teacher of this wisdom for Jesus, which he nourished by the Word of God. We can

imagine how Joseph taught the child Jesus to listen to the Holy Scriptures, especially accompanying him on the Sabbath to the synagogue in Nazareth ...

St. Luke tells us referring to Jesus: "The grace of God was upon Him". Here certainly the part reserved to St. Joseph is more limited ... But it would be a grave mistake to think that a father and a mother do nothing to educate their children to grow in the grace of God. The mission of St. Joseph is certainly unique and unrepeatable, because Jesus is unique. However, in his guarding Jesus, educating Him to grow in years, wisdom and grace, he is a model for all educators, especially for parents. St. Joseph is the model educator and father, the model for "dads" (Francis, 2014).

THE WISDOM OF JESUS

The wisdom of young Jesus is related in the Gospel of Luke, when He is twelve years of age. This account is known as the *Finding of Jesus in the Temple*. Every year, Jewish men were required by the Law to attend three feasts in Jerusalem, which were: Passover, Pentecost, and Tabernacles. Women and children could attend these feasts if they wished but were not required to. In the Gospel, both Joseph and Mary travelled to Jerusalem for Passover every year, and on this occasion, Jesus was with them:

Now His parents went to Jerusalem every year at the Feast of the Passover. And when He became twelve, they went up there according to the custom of the Feast (Luke 2:41-42 NASB).

The Bible reveals that after the Passover celebrations, Joseph and Mary left Jerusalem only to discover that their Son was not part of their caravan. The men and women traveled in separate groups, the young children with their mothers. Jesus, however, was already twelve years old, so He would have been in Joseph's large group of men. After travelling for one day, Joseph realized that Jesus was not in his group, so he assumed that He was with His mother, however He was not. After realizing that Jesus was not among their relatives, they journeyed with haste back to Jerusalem. How they blamed themselves for the losing of their Son.

> ... and as they were returning, ... the boy Jesus stayed behind in Jerusalem. But His parents were unaware of it, but supposed Him to be in the caravan, and went a day's journey; and they began looking for Him among their relatives and acquaintances. When they did not find Him, they returned to Jerusalem looking for Him. Then, after three days they found Him in the Temple, sitting in the midst of the teachers, both listening to them and asking them questions. And all who heard Him were amazed at His understanding and His answers (Luke 2:44-48 NASB).

> Most holy Mary and St. Joseph found themselves overwhelmed with self-reproach at their remissness in watching over their most holy Son and blamed themselves for His absence ... During all these three days St. Joseph, had suffered unspeakable sorrow and affliction, searching for his Son, his sincere and exquisite love for the divine Child made him so anxious and solicitous to find Him, that he allowed himself no time to care for his own nourishment so

long as his Son was lost. (M. Agreda, 1912, p. 36, 37, 42).

The relevance of this event in the life of St. Joseph is often overlooked and seen in passing, as Jesus shows Himself as a wise but respectful boy. Indeed, this mention in the Bible gives three hidden agendas, which each concerning a member of the Holy Family: God's presence among the scholars, Mary's intercession, and obedience to St. Joseph.

GOD AMONG MEN

The first agenda is glorifying the Christ child who demonstrated His deep and holy wisdom and understanding concerning matters of faith and logic. The Gospel of St. Luke reveals that He sat among the scholars and listened to their words, then gave His own opinions and observations. He amazed everyone with His profound insights, and even the teachers in the Temple were astounded by His words! In reading this there is a feeling of awe and wonder as Jesus astounded the group of learned men:

> After three days they found Him in the Temple, sitting in the midst of the teachers, both listening to them and asking them questions. And all who heard Him were amazed at His understanding and His answers. When they saw Him, they were astonished; and His mother said to Him, "Son, why have You treated us this way? Behold, Your father and I have been anxiously looking for You (Luke 2:46-48 NASB)."

When reading this encounter of the Lord among His people, in this case the adolescent Jesus among the teachers, the connection can be made to the Old Testament account of Abraham. In this story, the Holy Trinity came to Abraham as three men who spoke as one. They sat in his tent and he recognized these men as being God, calling them "My Lord". He even bowed down to them. To passersby these men were nothing special, but, they were the Holy Trinity, personally conversing with the Patriarch Abraham, sitting in his midst (Genesis 18:1). So too did God come in the Person of the young Jesus, who sat among the scholars and conversed. However, they had not recognized this boy as their Lord, yet He sat with them and left them full of wonder. Anna and Simeon however, twelve years earlier, *did* recognize Him in the Temple.

MATERNAL INTERCESSION

The second agenda is the role of Mary as mother and a glimpse of her role as intercessor. Her heart was breaking when she discovered that Jesus was missing. She experienced anxiety and heartache as she frantically searched for her Son. The grief was almost unbearable, as it is for many mothers who have lost their children. Did her son simply get lost in the crowds? Had He been kidnapped? Where was He? Jerusalem was a big place for rural people such as Mary and Joseph, and to retrace their steps would be agonizing. St. Joseph and the Blessed Virgin may be envisioned speaking the words of the Magdalene after she found the body of Jesus missing from the tomb years later:

> "And they said to her, "Woman, why are you weeping?" She said to them, "Because they have taken away my Lord, and I do not know where they have laid Him (John 20:13 NASB)."

When Mary and Joseph finally found their Son, it was Mary who first rushed to Jesus, telling Him of the anguish they felt when they discovered He was missing. Embracing Him she asked why He had done this to them, sighing her relief at finding Him.

> When they saw Him, they were astonished; and His mother said to Him, "Son, why have You treated us this way? Behold, Your father and I have been anxiously looking for You (Luke 2:48 NASB)."

Since it was Mary who spoke to Jesus, she was shown as intercessor and spoke on behalf of both Joseph and herself. She expressed to Jesus the sorrow and affliction they felt and petitioned Him as to why He had left them. She brought not only her grief to her Son, but Joseph's as well. Joseph felt Mary's pain and relief equally, but he allowed her to rush to their Son first so that she may embrace Him. Should one not also allow Mary to be their own intercessor, just as Joseph had, placing before her one's sorrows and anxieties? Our Lady, with a maternal heart, feels the sorrows of the children of God, and understands their needs, so who better to present them to Jesus than His own mother?

PATERNAL AUTHORITY

After Mary spoke to her Son, the third agenda is given concerning St. Joseph. Jesus' answer to His parents was simple, and some at first glance think His answer to be one of admonishment or disrespect towards His earthly father Joseph, however the opposite is true.

> And He said to them, "Why is it that you were looking for Me? Did you not know that I had to be in My Father's house (Luke 2:49 NASB)?"

Some would argue that this response is to be taken as a reproach for Joseph, that Jesus did not recognize the authority of Joseph's fatherhood over Him, but only that of God. Yet, would this not be a breach of the Fourth Commandment given to Moses by God Himself? Jesus did not commit this sin or any sin. Rather, Jesus was infused with so much knowledge and love of God the Father that He felt at home in the Temple, doing God's work and discussing Him. He was answering in a sincere and direct way. This was by no means a reprimand, after all, isn't God the Father of Abraham, Isaac, Jacob, Moses and David? Is He not also the Father of Joseph and Jesus? Joseph, as with the scholars in the Temple, was called to a life of service to God.

St. Joseph was happy not only for having found his Son, but for having found Him at the Temple, with Jesus demonstrating that our desire should be to seek Him and to do the will of the Father. His son was becoming a young man of wisdom and deep understanding, growing in grace before God the Father. Mother Cecelia Baij reveals the joy of St. Joseph upon finding Jesus at the Jerusalem Temple:

> Joseph experienced joy upon seeing Jesus and listening to His words of wisdom imparted to the men of learning at the Temple. He saw how they all wondered at the graciousness and wisdom of this Youth, and remarked to himself:

> "Behold, now my Jesus will be known and accepted for what He is, the true Messiah. Since He is expounding the Scriptures to them so wonderfully and wisely and is also making it so evident to them that the Messiah has indeed come, they will necessarily love Him (C. Baij, 1997, pg. 291, 292).

Joseph's position of family head is asserted with the closing verses, along with yet another mention of Mary's treasury, which is her Immaculate Heart:

128

And He went down with them and came to Nazareth, and He continued in subjection to them; and His mother treasured all these things in her heart. And Jesus kept increasing in wisdom and stature, and in favour with God and men (Luke 2:51-52 NASB).

Pope Benedict XVI and Pope Leo XIII reflect:

In the Gospel of St. Luke, Joseph appears in one more episode, when he goes to Jerusalem and lives the anguish of losing the Son Jesus. St. Luke describes the anxious search and the wonder at finding Him in the Temple, but even greater is the astonishment at hearing the mysterious words: "How is it that you sought me? Did you not know that I must be in my Father's house?" (St. Luke 2:49.) This twofold question of the Son of God helps us to understand the mystery of Joseph's paternity. Reminding His own parents of the primacy of the one He calls "My Father," Jesus affirms the primacy of the will of God over every other will, and reveals to Joseph the profound truth of his role: He too is called to be a disciple of Jesus, dedicating his existence to the service of the Son of God and of the Virgin Mother, in obedience to the Heavenly Father (Benedict XVI, July 2010).

Joseph shines among all mankind by the most august dignity, since by Divine Will, he was the guardian of the Son of God and reputed as His father among men. Hence it came about that the Word of God was humbly subject to Joseph, that He obeyed him, and that He rendered to him all those offices that children are bound to render to their parents (Leo XIII, 1889).

After the losing and finding of Jesus in Jerusalem, there are no details recorded in the Bible about the life of the Holy Family until Christ is a fully-grown man. These years in between were simpler and quieter than the preceding ones, with Jesus and St. Joseph working side by side at their trade. After this period, there are only brief references to St. Joseph:

> "Where did this man get this wisdom and these miraculous powers? Is not this the carpenter's son (Matthew 13:54-55 NASB)?"

> "We have found Him of whom Moses in the Law and also the Prophets wrote—Jesus of Nazareth, the son of Joseph (John 1:45 NASB)."

> They were saying, "Is not this Jesus, the son of Joseph, whose father and mother we know (John 6:42 NASB)?"

CHAPTER 10: THE DIGNITY OF WORK

This chapter speaks of St. Joseph's role of carpenter, provider for his family, and Jesus working at his side.

> And I have found that nothing is better than for a man to rejoice in his work, and that this is his portion (Ecclesiastes 3:22 DRV).

ST. JOSEPH THE WORKER

The Bible reveals that St. Joseph was a carpenter, but did he work only with wood? The word "faber," used in the Latin scriptures when defining Joseph's occupation, was a general term applied to a craftsman in any material; this could be one who works with wood, stone, iron, or even precious metals. St. Hilarion, St. Isidore, and St. Bede believed that Joseph was an ironsmith and wrote in their commentaries on the Gospels that Jesus was the Son of "the smith who subdues iron with fire."

The great saints Justin Martyr, Thomas Aquinas, and John Chrysostom, however, held the opinion that Joseph was in fact a worker of wood, as was Jesus:

St. Justin Martyr:

> Jesus came to John, being reputed the son of Joseph, the carpenter, or worker in wood, and He Himself was reckoned to be a carpenter; for while He dwelt amongst men He had performed carpenter's work, making ploughs and yokes, teaching us to live just lives free from idleness (E. Thompson, 1891, pg. 100).

St. Thomas Aquinas:

> Jesus was reputed to be the son of Joseph, who was not a forger of iron but a worker in wood (E. Thompson, 1891, pg. 100).

St. John Chrysostom

> Therefore, Mary was espoused to a carpenter, because Jesus, the Spouse of the Church, was to work the salvation of the world by the wood of the Cross (E. Thompson, 1891, pg. 100).

The accepted idea is that Joseph was truly a carpenter who worked with wood, but also worked with other materials on the side. The earliest art depicting Joseph shows him holding carpentry tools, but he may be envisioned working with both wood and iron. He could be called on to build furniture, help build a neighbor's house, replace locks, or hang doors. What Joseph did for a living isn't as important as how he did it. Certainly, Joseph was known as being not only a fine workman, but also a man of integrity. Joseph was a master of his trade and put care into the work he did for people, and the people of Nazareth knew this. They knew that he was not at all greedy, or unfair, but was an honest man to do business with. Mother Cecelia Baij reveals this:

> Saint Joseph performed all his work exceptionally well, and everybody was always impressed by it. Joseph only took what was offered to him for his labour. He left the amount of pay up to them, and he received it from them with thanks, as if it were a gift rather than payment owed to him. … In his little workshop, Joseph would always make time for prayer and would often lower himself to the ground

and make a complete oblation of himself to God (C. Baij, 1997, pg. 232).

In the encyclical *Quamquam Pluries*, Pope Leo XIII shows the dignity of St. Joseph the Worker and praises him:

For Joseph, of royal blood, united by marriage to the greatest and holiest of women, reputed the father of the Son of God, passed his life in labour, and won by the toil of the artisan the needful support of his family. It is, then, true that the condition of the lowly has nothing shameful in it, and the work of the labourer is not only not dishonouring, but can, if virtue be joined to it, be singularly ennobled. Joseph, content with his slight possessions, bore the trials consequent on a fortune so slender, with greatness of soul, in imitation of his Son, who having put on the form of a slave, being the Lord of life, subjected Himself of His own free-will to the spoliation and loss of everything (Leo XIII, 1889).

JESUS THE YOUNG CARPENTER

After several years in Nazareth, the transition in the life of Christ was at hand and He was to engage fully in manual work at His father's side. In the years leading up to this, He spent most of His time with Mary in the home of Nazareth while His father worked to provide for the family. As Jesus grew into manhood, He became more involved with St. Joseph's work in the family's carpentry shop. A scene is given by Servant of God Mother Cecilia Baij, and a reflection by Pope St. John Paul II and Pope Francis:

To see Jesus present in his shop made Joseph's heart leap for joy ... Turning to Jesus, Joseph said: "Oh my dear Son, you already know that my desire is to be at Your service, but the Heavenly Father has decreed otherwise. In obedience to Him, I shall have command over You. Nevertheless, I shall do so only to fulfill the Will of God." In reply, Jesus encouraged Joseph to make his demands freely, as they were both obliged to carry out the designs of the Heavenly Father. The Divine Youth always stood by, ready to be of service, and ... He wanted to be commanded by Joseph, and, thereby, practice humility and submissiveness (C. Baij, 1997, pg. 271).

Work was the daily expression of love in the life of the Family of Nazareth. The Gospel specifies the kind of work Joseph did to support his family: he was a carpenter. This simple word sums up Joseph's entire life. ... Having learned the work of His presumed father, Jesus was known as "the carpenter's son." If the Family of Nazareth is an example and model for human families, in the order of salvation and holiness, so too, by analogy, is Jesus' work at the side of Joseph the carpenter ... At the workbench where he plied his trade together with Jesus, Joseph brought human work closer to the mystery of the Redemption (John Paul II, 1989).

In the Gospel of St. Matthew, one of the times when Jesus returns to His native region, Nazareth, and speaks in the synagogue, the Gospel underlines His fellow villagers' astonishment at His wisdom, and the question they ask one another: "is not this the carpenter's son?" (13:55). Jesus enters our history, He comes into our midst, being born of Mary by the work of God, but with the presence of St. Joseph, the legal father who guards and teaches Him. Jesus was born and lived in a family, learning from St. Joseph

134

the carpenter's trade, sharing with him his commitment, hard work and satisfaction, as well as each day's difficulties. This calls to mind for us the dignity and importance of work ... Work is part of the plan of God's love; we are called to cultivate and safeguard all the goods of creation and in this way, we participate in the work of creation (Francis, 2013).

There is nothing better for a man than to eat and drink and tell himself that his labour is good. This also I have seen that it is from the hand of God (Ecclesiastes 2:24 NASB).

PART THREE: THE COMMUNION OF SAINTS

And another angel came, and stood before the altar, having a golden censer; and there was given to him much incense, that he should offer of the prayers of all saints upon the golden altar, which is before the throne of God (Revelation 8:3-4 DRV).

CHAPTER 1: THE SERVANT DEPARTS

This chapter speaks of St. Joseph being consumed by divine love in his final days, his final words to Jesus and Mary, his holy death in their company, and the carrying of his blessed soul to Limbo.

As Jesus entered manhood, He and Joseph continued in their close relationship; conversing, praying, and working side by side as father and son. St. Alphonsus reflects:

> The two disciples, going to Emmaus, (Luke 24:13-31) were inflamed with divine love by the few moments which they spent in company with our Saviour, and by His words. What flames of holy love must not, then, have been enkindled in the heart of St. Joseph, who for thirty years conversed with Jesus Christ, and listened to His words of eternal life; who observed the perfect example which Jesus gave of humility and patience, and saw the promptness with which He obeyed and helped him in his labours, and all that was needed for the household (A. Liguori, 2017)!

CONSUMED BY DIVINE LOVE

Joseph was constantly faithful in his devotion to his Lord and Lady and would often experience ecstasies as a reward; his heart constantly aflame with love that it consumed his whole being. As he became more and more afflicted by love, he began to yearn for the day of his death, while asking the Lord to envelop him completely in this fiery love. This divine burning grew so intense that it began to radiate outwardly in Joseph's physical appearance. During the latter days of Joseph's life, Jesus would often visit with him, caring for and encouraging him, especially during the violent bursts of ecstatic love within his body and soul.

Mother Cecelia Baij and Venerable Maria de Agreda reveal these moments:

> The love of God attained such an intensity within Joseph, that his body was affected by it. His heart became as a volcano of fiery divine love, so that he would often exclaim: "Oh, God of love! Put an end to my life! Oh, if this fire of love now burning in my breast would only consume me completely!" Joseph began to have the desire for death by being consumed with divine love. ... Joseph's heart was on fire, his body was radiant, and his eyes sparkled. Mary was delighted as she looked at Joseph, for he seemed to be more like a creature of Heaven than of earth (C. Baij, 1997, pg. 307).

> Joseph, in his final years, was weakened from the fire of his ardent love which was so vehement, that the flights and ecstasies of his most pure soul would often have burst the bounds of his body if the Lord, who vouchsafed them, had not strengthened and comforted him against these agonies of love (M. Agreda, 1912, p. 143).

FINAL MOMENTS

> Blessed are the dead, who die in the Lord. From henceforth now, saith the Spirit, that they may rest from their labours; for their works follow them (Revelation 14:13 DRA).

It is widely held that St. Joseph passed away in Nazareth at the age of sixty-three. His death occurred while Jesus was still at home, before He departed and began His public ministry. After the event of the Losing and Finding of Jesus in the Temple, Joseph is no longer active in the Bible, whereas our Lady is still present throughout the rest of Christ's life. The most notable examples are the Wedding Feast of Cana, the Crucifixion, and Pentecost. These examples mention Mary but not her blessed spouse, who surely would have been at her side for these events. At the Crucifixion scene, the mother of Christ stands at the foot of the cross with her cousin Mary, and John (the beloved apostle) to whom Jesus entrusts His mother. Had Joseph been alive, Jesus would have no need to place Mary into the care of His beloved friend.

One might ask, since Jesus had the power to resurrect the dead, such as He did for His friend Lazarus and others, why did He not do the same for His father on earth? Jesus did not do this for Joseph because Joseph had fulfilled his mission on earth – to guard, nurture and raise the Son of God into manhood. Joseph had indeed accomplished what the Lord had asked of him and fulfilled it with the utmost love, honour, and humility. The mystics reveal that in Joseph's final days, he experienced intense ecstasies and the comfort of the angels, with Jesus and Mary at his side. Mother Cecelia Baij, Blessed Anne Catherine Emmerich, and Venerable Maria de Agreda relate:

> During the final period of his life, St. Joseph was privileged to hear the singing of the angels, announcing to him his blessed departure being near at hand. This news gave him great joy and consolation of spirit. The Saviour was at his side to provide comfort with His divine words, and Mary would also sit with him (C. Baij, 1997, p.335).

> When Joseph was dying, Mary sat at the head of his bed, holding him in her arms. Jesus stood just below

her near Joseph's breast. The whole room was brilliant with light and full of angels (A. Emmerich, 1953, pg. 330).

St. Joseph's noble soul had been purified more and more each day in the affliction of divine love. The days before his death, St. Joseph enjoyed the company of Jesus and Mary and by command of the Lord the holy angels played celestial music, mixing their hymns of praise with the benedictions of the Saint, accompanied by the sweetest fragrances, to comfort the dying Saint. On the day before he died, being inflamed with divine love, he was wrapped in an ecstasy in which he clearly saw the mysteries of the Incarnation and Redemption, and the militant Church with all its Sacraments and mysteries. When St. Joseph issued from this ecstasy his face shone with wonderful splendour and his soul was transformed by his vision of the essence of God (M. Agreda, 1912, p. 151, 152).

THE FINAL WORDS OF ST. JOSEPH

Regarding the final sweet words of the carpenter of Nazareth, Mother Cecelia Baij and Venerable Maria de Agreda reveal that Joseph, second only to the Blessed Virgin Mary in holiness among God's creatures, begged forgiveness of Jesus and Mary for any wrongs he may have committed as father and spouse. He gave thanks to them for all their love, and especially thanked Christ for His future sufferings that would save mankind. Mother Cecelia Baij reveals St. Joseph's gratitude:

Joseph begged Jesus and Mary to forgive him for any deficiencies on his part as father and husband. ... He thanked them for all the love that they manifested towards him, for their patience, and for all the graces that he obtained from them. ... Finally, he gave thanks to the Saviour for everything He already suffered, and that He would suffer in the future, to accomplish the great work of the redemption of mankind (C. Baij, 1997, pg. 337).

Joseph then blessed and praised Mary while telling her that he looked forward to the day of their reunion in Heaven. St. Joseph's love for his spouse was unparalleled to that of any spouse in the history of creation, and here, in his final moments on this earth, he prayed that all generations would indeed call her blessed (St. Luke 1:46-55). Venerable Maria de Agreda reveals the sincere words of St. Joseph, to the spouse he would soon leave behind:

"Blessed art thou among all women. Let angels and men praise Thee; let all the generations know, praise and exalt thy dignity; and may the Most High be eternally praised for having created thee so pleasing in His eyes and in the sight of all the blessed spirits. I hope to enjoy thy sight in the heavenly fatherland" (M. Agreda, 1912, p. 152).

Then, turning toward Christ his Son, the ever-humble Saint attempted to kneel before Him and beg forgiveness for any mistakes he may have made while raising the Son of God as his own. Joseph adored and exalted his Son, acknowledging Him as his God, asked Him for a final blessing, and gave thanks to Him for choosing him to be the husband of Mary, who brought him into the mystery of salvation history. Venerable Maria de Agreda speaks of these moments between father and son:

Then this man of God, turning toward Christ, in reverence, wished to kneel before Him. But the sweetest Jesus, coming near, received him in His arms, were, reclining his head upon them, Joseph said:

"My highest Lord and God, Son of the eternal Father, give Thy blessing to Thy servant; pardon the faults which I have committed in Thy service and interactions. I extol and magnify Thee and render heartfelt thanks to Thee for having chosen me to be the spouse of Thy true mother; let Thy greatness and glory be my thanksgiving for all eternity" (M. Agreda, 1912, p. 153).

THE HOLY DEATH OF ST. JOSEPH

After Joseph spoke his final words, he received the blessing of Christ as well as his next mission, to be carried out in Limbo, until the time of Christ's ascension into Heaven. Venerable Maria de Agreda and Mother Cecelia Baij reveal this mission given to Joseph as well as the moment of his death in the company of his beloved Jesus and Mary:

The Redeemer of the world gave him His benediction, saying: "My father, rest in peace and in the grace of thy eternal Father and Mine; and to the Prophets and Saints, who await thee in Limbo, bring the joyful news of the approach of their redemption."
At these words of Jesus, and reclining in His arms, the most fortunate Saint Joseph expired and the Lord Himself closed his eyes. At the same time the multitude of the angels intoned hymns of praise in loud and harmonious voices (M. Agreda, 1912, pg.153).

The Saviour held him and spoke to him of the glory, love, and generosity of His Heavenly Father. These words penetrated deeply into the soul of the dying Joseph, and they inflamed him still more with love for God. Since the final moment of Joseph's life had arrived, the Son of God then invited Joseph's blessed soul to depart from his body, so that it might be taken up in His own holy hands, and from there committed to the angels who were to escort it into Limbo. In response to this sweet invitation, the blissful Joseph breathed forth his soul in an act of love for God with the sweetest names of Jesus and Mary on his lips (C. Baij, 1997, pg. 328).

JESUS CONSOLES HIS MOTHER

Jesus, in seeing that His mother was grieved at the loss of her blessed Spouse, comforted her and promised her that Joseph will be honoured in the next life unlike any other man before him. Venerable Maria de Agreda reveals the words of the Saviour to His mother:

> "My mother, the merits of Joseph are acceptable in My eyes. I have assigned him a place among the princes of My people, so high that he will be the admiration of the angels and will cause them and all men to break forth in highest praise. With none of the human born shall I do as with thy spouse" (M. Agreda, 1912, pg. 151).

THE CARRYING OF JOSEPH'S SOUL TO LIMBO

After his holy death, Jesus entrusted the soul of Joseph to the care of the angels and commanded them to bring him to the place of honour prepared for him in Limbo, where he was to remain until the day of Christ's ascension into Heaven. Mother Cecelia Baij and Venerable Maria de Agreda reveal:

> The Saviour now took Joseph's soul up into His holy hands and allowed His Mother to behold it, so that she might be consoled. She saw her spouse's most perfect soul, so adorned with virtue and grace and so rich in merits and she rejoiced over the holiness of her blessed Joseph's soul (C. Baij, 1997, pg. 339).

> By command of the Lord the angels carried Joseph's most holy soul to the gathering place of the Patriarchs and Prophets, where it was immediately recognized by all as clothed in the splendors of incomparable grace, as the putative father and the intimate friend of the Redeemer, worthy of highest veneration ... His arrival spread joy in this countless gathering of the saints by the announcement of their speedy rescue (M. Agreda, 1912, pg. 153).

Saints Alphonsus de Liguori and Francis de Sales reflect on the death of St. Joseph:

> "Precious in the eyes of the Lord is the death of His faithful ones" (Psalm 116:15). After having faithfully served Jesus and Mary, Saint Joseph reached the end of his life in the house at Nazareth. There, surrounded by angels, assisted by Jesus Christ the King of angels, and by Mary, his spouse, who placed themselves at each side of his poor bed, filled with the peace of paradise, he departed from this miserable life. Who shall ever be able to understand the sweetness, the consolation, the blessed hope, the acts of resignation, the flames of charity which the

words of eternal life coming alternately from the lips of Jesus and Mary, breathed into the soul of Joseph at the end of his life (A. Liguori, 2017)?

> St. Joseph, who had loved so much in his life, could not die but of love; ... and having already performed the duty which was required in the childhood of Jesus, what remained was that he should say ... to the Son, "O my child! As your Heavenly Father put Your tender body into my hands the day You came into this world, so do I render up my soul into *Your* hands, this day of my departure *out* of the world." Such, as I conceive, was the death of this great patriarch, a man elected to perform the most tender and loving offices that ever were or shall be performed to the Son of God, save those that were done by his sacred spouse, the true natural mother of the said Son (E. Thompson, 1953, pg. 406).

St. Joseph, having completed the mission entrusted to him on earth, was then ready for the next stage in his service to God; he was to be a herald and comfort to the Patriarchs of Limbo – announcing their coming redemption. After the Ascension of Christ, he would then be brought to Heaven where he would take on another role in God's plan – that of the intercessor.

CHAPTER 2: THE SLEEPING PRINCE

This chapter speaks of the beautiful body of St. Joseph, and the place known as Limbo.

After his soul was taken into Christ's hands and given to the care of the angels, St. Joseph's body was prepared for burial by Mary. While preparing the body, such bright light radiated from it that only Joseph's face could be seen by the Blessed Virgin. After being prepared for procession and burial, the light dimmed somewhat so that people could behold him and marvel at how beautiful he was. His body so lifelike in appearance, and emitting the fragrance of sanctity, was admired by those who took part in the burial procession, as confirmed by Venerable Maria de Agreda and Maria Cecelia Baij:

> Her spouse having thus passed away, Mary began to prepare his body for burial. No other hands touched him other than those of his spouse and those of the holy angels, who assisted her. God enveloped the body of saint Joseph in a wonderful light, which hid all except his face, with the sweetest fragrance coming from his body which remained so beautiful and lifelike; the neighboring people came to see it and were filled with admiration. Accompanied by the Redeemer, His most blessed Mother, and a great multitude of angels, and escorted by their friends and many others, the sacred body of the most glorious Saint Joseph was borne to the common burying place (M. Agreda, 1912, pg. 154).

> His body was surrounded by a wonderful radiance and emitted a delightful scent. His attractiveness remained unchanged, and he seemed truly to resemble an angel of paradise. Everyone who saw

him was moved to venerate him, their hearts all deeply touched and moved to tears (C. Baij, 1997, pg. 339).

It is believed that after Joseph's happy and holy passing, his body was entombed in the foothills of the Mount of Olives in Jerusalem. There it rested while his soul was in the Bosom of Abraham, Limbo.

LIMBO: THE BOSOM OF ABRAHAM

Joseph's soul was taken to Limbo by the angels to announce to the Prophets and Patriarchs of the Old Covenant the Gospel of Christ and their forthcoming release to Heaven, after the Passion, Death, Resurrection and Ascension of Jesus.

> In the moments before St. Joseph's death, the Blessed Trinity commissioned him to be the messenger of the Saviour to the holy Patriarchs and Prophets of Limbo; and commanded him to prepare them for their issuing forth from this bosom of Abraham to eternal rest and happiness (M. Agreda, 1912, pg. 151).

In the Gospel of St. John, Jesus reveals that He will return to His "Father's house" where He will "go to prepare a place" for His apostles and that "no one may come to the Father except through Me" (John 14:2-6). Jesus is the gateway to the Eternal Paradise of Heaven since it is He who conquers the corruption of death, but does not the Old Testament reveal that Elijah, who died long before Jesus came to conquer death, was carried up to Heaven in a chariot of fire?

> And it came to pass, when the Lord would take up Elias into heaven by a whirlwind . . . behold a fiery chariot and fiery horses parted them both asunder:

and Elias went up by a whirlwind into heaven (4 Kings 2:1, 11 DRV).

The prophets of the Old Testament were taken up to Limbo, which may be likened to a type of waiting room to get into Heaven. Those who had not known Jesus Christ but who led righteous lives went to this place. This was the place of the dead, of those who had died before Jesus Himself was crucified and died, only to rise from His tomb.

The word "Limbo" refers to the edge of a hem on a garment, the border, and that is why this term is used to describe this place of waiting. The Bible itself does not use this word, but the place has been referred to as the Bosom of Abraham. This place was separated by a chasm with the righteous on one side and the wicked on the other. Jesus Himself refers to this place in the Parable of the Unjust Steward:

> Now the poor man died and was carried away by the angels to Abraham's Bosom; and the rich man also died and was buried. In Hades he lifted his eyes, being in torment, and saw Abraham far away and Lazarus in his bosom (Luke 16:22-24 NASB).

CHAPTER 3: CROWN OF ETERNAL LIFE

This chapter speaks of the possible bodily assumption of St. Joseph.

> Be faithful until death, and I will give you the crown
> of life (Revelation 2:10 NASB).

Of all the saints in Christendom, the only pair of whom there are no first-class relics are the Blessed Virgin Mary and St. Joseph. The lack of bodily relics of Mary is attributed to her assumption into Heaven, body and soul, which is one of the great Marian Dogmas of the Church. This tradition has been popularly believed from the earliest days of the Church but was not officially defined as dogma until November 1, 1950 by Venerable Pope Pius XII. The same reasoning is applied to the lack of bodily relics of St. Joseph, Virgin-Father of Christ and Chaste Spouse of Mary.

THE INCORRUPT BODY OF ST. JOSEPH

Many hold the belief that St. Joseph's soul was, after his sojourn in Limbo, reunited with his body and taken to Heaven on the day of the Ascension of Christ. Others believe that only his soul is in Heaven, and that his body still lies incorrupt in some hidden tomb awaiting discovery. This was the belief of Father Paul of Moll, a miracle worker in the 19th century who vaguely stated that some (unnamed) saint has seen the incorrupt body in a tomb:

> In an ecstasy, a saint has seen the body of St. Joseph
> preserved intact in a tomb, the site of which is yet
> unknown. The more the glorious Spouse of the most
> Blessed Virgin is honoured, the sooner will the
> finding of his body take place, which will be a day of
> great joy for the Church (E. Speybrouck, 1979).

It is not known who has seen the incorrupt body of St. Joseph, although Blessed Ann Catherine Emmerich did say she thought she saw it in one of her visions, though she was not sure; perhaps she is who the "saint" Fr. Paul of Moll is speaking of? There is no solid evidence, at this time, to support the idea of the incorrupt body of St. Joseph still waiting to be found and no traditions have ever held this.

> After St. Joseph's death, his hands were crossed on his breast, he was wrapped from head to foot in a white sheet, laid in a narrow casket, and placed in a very beautiful tomb, the gift of a good man. I saw the angels following in the funeral procession. Joseph's remains were afterward removed by the Christians to Bethlehem, and interred. I think I can see him still lying there incorrupt (A. Emmerich, 1953, pg. 330).

Perhaps this transferral of St. Joseph's remains happened before the end of Christ's life, and his body did remain incorrupt until his possible assumption?

THE ASSUMPTION OF ST. JOSEPH

The subject of the possibility of the bodily Assumption of St. Joseph into Heaven has been discussed through the centuries. However, at this time there is no definite, dogmatic, teaching of the Church regarding this. However, many saints and mystics have attested to their belief in the Assumption of Joseph. This is the pious belief of such saints as Francis de Sales and Bernardino of Siena, along with the mystic Mother Cecelia Baij, and alluded to by St. Pope John XXIII:

154

When our Lord descended into Limbo, St. Joseph spoke to Him thus:

"Oh, my Lord! Please remember that when You came down from Heaven upon this earth, I welcomed You into my abode and family. Receive me now into Yours. While You lived on earth, I carried You in my arms. Take me now into Your own. It was my concern to provide for You and watch over You during Your mortal existence. Take care of me now and lead me into eternal life."

How could we doubt that our Lord raised glorious St. Joseph up into Heaven, body and soul? For he had the honour and grace of carrying Him so often in his blessed arms, arms in which our Lord took so much pleasure. Truly, St. Joseph is in Heaven, both body and soul. Of this there can be no doubt (F. Sales, 2017).

Although it is not defined dogma, we are free to believe that Jesus honoured His adopted father in the same way as He has honoured His Blessed Mother. In the same way that Mary was to be assumed into Heaven, Jesus, it is thought, glorified Joseph on the day of the Resurrection or Ascension. In this way, all the Holy Family — Jesus, Mary and Joseph — who lived together on earth would reign together in Heaven (B. Albizensci, 2017).

When the Saviour of the world gloriously and victoriously arose from the dead ... He thereafter proceeded to deliver and to take with Him from Limbo, those souls which had been confined there. St. Joseph's glorified soul was, by the power of God, again reunited to his blessed body ... Joseph made his entry into Heaven together with the Saviour on the occasion of His remarkable Ascension. There the Saint now occupies, in virtue of his virginity and great purity of soul, a most distinguished throne near to the unspotted Lamb of God (C. Baij, 1997, pg. 340).

We name one of the most intimate persons in Christ's life: Joseph of Nazareth – his putative father and custodian. It corresponds to him – we may piously believe – the honour and the privilege of Jesus allowing him to admirably accompany Him on the path to Heaven (on the day of His Ascension) and to sing the first notes of the never-ending hymn, "Te Deum" (John XXIII, 1960).

PRESENT ONLY IN SPIRIT?

One may feel validated in the belief of the possible Assumption of St. Joseph by looking to the apparitions of the 20th century, one example being the apparitions at Fatima, Portugal. When St. Joseph appeared at Fatima, Portugal, to bless the world on October 13, 1917, holding the Child Jesus and standing next to the Virgin Mary, would he just have been some type of "ghost" holding the flesh and blood Jesus standing next to flesh and blood Blessed Virgin? One could argue that it does not make sense that the Earthly Trinity: Jesus, Mary and Joseph – who were so closely united on Earth – would be hindered in their union in Heaven. Servant of God Lucia dos Santos recalls:

> We saw, beside the sun, St. Joseph with the Child Jesus and our Lady clothed in white with a blue mantle. St. Joseph and the Child Jesus appeared to

156

bless the world, for they traced the Sign of the Cross with their hands (L. Santos, 2007, pg. 183).

CROWN OF LIFE

If ever a man existed who deserves the splendor of Heaven it is St. Joseph, the "just man" (St. Matthew 1:19) who lived such an honourable and holy life. He is united with his beloved spouse Mary and with Jesus the Eternal Son, whom he raised as his own flesh and blood. His trials have long passed, his anxieties have been calmed, and his rough hands, which supported his family, have been soothed by the Divine Healer, Who crowns his achievements and tribulations with everlasting life.

> ... when he hath been proved, he shall receive a crown of life, which God hath promised to them that love Him (James 1:12 DRV).

St. Bernardino reflects:

> It is beyond doubt that Christ did not deny to Joseph in Heaven that intimacy, respect, and high honour which He showed to him as to a father during His own human life, but rather completed and perfected it. Justifiably the words of the Lord should be applied to him, 'Enter into the joy of your Lord.' Although it is the joy of eternal happiness that comes into the heart of man, the Lord prefers to say to him 'enter into joy'. The mystical implication is that this joy is not just inside man, but surrounds him everywhere and absorbs him, as if he were plunged in an infinite abyss (B. Albizensci, 2017).

CHAPTER 4: DEFENDER OF THE CHURCH

This chapter speaks of the missions of St. Michael the Archangel and St. Joseph Patron of the Church in defending the Mystical Body of Christ.

... And I say to thee: That thou art Peter; and upon this rock I will build my church, and the gates of hell shall not prevail against it (Matthew 16:18 DRV).

POPE LEO XIII & ST. MICHAEL THE ARCHANGEL

On October 13, 1884, Pope Leo XIII experienced something mystical and terrifying—something which would plague him with fear and worry regarding the welfare of none other than Holy Mother Church. After celebrating Mass in his private chapel with a group of cardinals and members of his household staff, as he was leaving the altar, the Pope suddenly froze in his steps, his face ashen white, with his gaze fixed upon the Tabernacle. After issuing forth from his ecstasy ten minutes later, and without explaining to anyone what had happened, he rushed into his office and immediately composed what is commonly known as the "St. Michael Prayer". He quickly instructed that this prayer, from then on, was to be said after all Low Masses worldwide. After giving these instructions, he related what happened.

It had been said that as he was about to leave the foot of the altar, he suddenly heard two voices—one gentle, the other harsh. The voices seemed to come from the direction of the Tabernacle. As he listened to the conversation, everything seemed to disappear from around him and all that existed were those two voices. He heard the voice of Satan who, in his pride, boasted to the other voice, belonging to our Lord, that if he were given one hundred years (seventy-five according to some sources) and given more power, he could bring about the destruction of the Holy Catholic

Church. Our Lord agreed to this, granting him the time and the power.

Now, one would ask, why would Jesus allow such a thing? Because He knows that the forces of Hell will never prevail against His church (Matthew 16:18) but the devil, being so full of pride, would never accept this. In the Bible it is shown, most notably in the Book of Revelation, that the devil is at war with St. Michael the Archangel and his Holy Army. It is because of this, that the Pope hurried to exhort the faithful to pray the following prayer, which is also of a prophetic nature, given here in its simplified form:

> Saint Michael the Archangel defend us in battle. Be our protection against the wickedness and snares of the devil. May God rebuke him, we humbly pray; and do thou, O Prince of the Heavenly Host – by the Power of God – cast into Hell, Satan and all the evil spirits, who prowl throughout the world seeking the ruin of souls. Amen (Michael Journal, 2017).

As seen in this prayer, Pope Leo XIII had insight into the future struggles of the Church and implored most fervently the assistance of the Archangel Michael. Without going into detail, one could say that since the vision of the Pope, the Church has been under attack both from the outside and from within.

POPE PIUS IX & ST. JOSEPH

In 1870 Pope Leo XIII's predecessor, Blessed Pius IX, issued *Quemadmodum Deus*. In this document, the reality of the Church coming under attack, from all sides and even from within, was made apparent. Pius IX, stricken with grief by the assaults against the Church decided to turn to St. Joseph, not only composing a prayer to him, but going one step further, and proclaiming St. Joseph to be the Patron of the Universal Church. This is no idle gesture in the eyes of those who truly love the Mystical Body of Christ, the One, Holy, Catholic and Apostolic Church.

> And now, in these most troublesome times, the Church is beset by enemies on every side, and is weighed down by calamities so heavy that ungodly men assert that the gates of Hell have at length prevailed against Her, the venerable prelates of the whole Catholic world have presented to the Sovereign Pontiff their own petitions and those of the faithful committed to their charge, praying that he would deign to constitute St. Joseph Patron of the Church. Accordingly, it has now pleased our Most Holy Sovereign, Pope Pius IX, to entrust himself and all the faithful to the Patriarch St. Joseph's most powerful patronage, to comply with the prelates' desire and has solemnly declared him Patron of the Catholic Church (Pius IX, 2017).

In this excerpt, it is seen that initially it was the people who wanted St. Joseph's help for the Church, who petitioned their bishops, who then approached the Holy Father. Humanity was crying out for St. Joseph's intercession. The Pope lamented that "the Church is beset by enemies on every side..." and this was all too obvious at the time as the 19th century brought much violence against the Catholic Church. At the time, the Franco-Prussian war was being fought; the Italian governments wanted to take over Rome which before then had always been under the Pope's authority; King Victor Emmanuel II waged open war against Pope Pius IX and the anti-clerical newspapers applauded the taking over of the Papal States.

This is one of the great reasons why Pius IX turned to Joseph, to protect the Papacy and the Church. The proclaiming of St. Joseph as Patron of the Catholic Church was no idle gesture. In times of calamity the papacy looked to him who had the duty of protecting none other than God the Son and His Blessed Mother. If one truly believes that the Church is the Mystical Body of Christ, then one must have a special devotion to St. Joseph who guards this Body. He resembles the cherub who held the flaming sword, appointed by God to guard the Garden of Eden. If it is held to be true that the Holy Father is the Vicar of Christ, then one must believe in the Church's pronouncement of St. Joseph being named Patron of the Catholic Church. When a Pope speaks, his are not meaningless words to be forgotten over the next generations but, rather, his words are binding.

> Amen I say to you, whatsoever you shall bind upon earth, shall be bound also in Heaven; and whatsoever you shall loose upon earth, shall be loosed also in Heaven (Matthew 18:18 DRV).

POPE LEO XIII & ST. JOSEPH

St. Joseph is pure, humble and obedient, whereas the devil and his followers are the far opposite. They know nothing of love or purity and since these attributes are a part of the embodiment of St. Joseph, the demons are afraid of him. The serpent who seduced in the Garden of Eden—the Dragon who makes war on the Church in the Book of Revelation, is terrified of all that is true and holy. The devil tempts Eve to disobey God because he is afraid of those who follow the Lord. By being afraid and at the same time too proud, the devil resorts to manipulation and seduction to divert Eve from what is good, with Adam falling with her. The downfall of Adam and Eve is the Serpent's triumph.

Satan, in the guise of the Dragon of Revelation, makes war on the wondrous Woman Clothed with the Sun and seeks to devour her Son and those who follow Him. The Dragon seeks to destroy what he does not know. He does not know love; therefore, he is afraid of it, seeking to eradicate it. Since the Church is the Mystical Body of Jesus Christ, which was instituted by Christ himself, the devil wants to destroy it. If he can conquer the Church, and those who are a part of it, he reigns triumphant.

Pope Leo XIII knew this and, even after going to St. Michael the Archangel, he still wanted reinforcement in the protection of the Catholic Church. In 1889 he composed the Encyclical *Quamquam Pluries,* concerning devotion to St. Joseph, who had previously been proclaimed Patron of the Church by Blessed Pope Pius IX. He called upon St. Joseph because no saint, save the Blessed Virgin Mary, is as holy, as valiant, and as powerful as he is. Just as Satan is afraid of the Immaculate one, so too is he terrified of her Blessed Spouse. St. Joseph is pure of heart, body, mind and intention. St. Joseph was a man, born of a woman, and yet he is holier than the angels themselves! The demons were once holy angels and their pride brought about their downfall, so seeing this man who is all holy and all obedient to God, scares them. How could a mere man attain such greatness and glory through God? Their pride will not allow them to see this man. They are blinded with rage and are confused as to why God chose to subject Himself as the Son of St. Joseph of Nazareth, a lowly carpenter, a mortal.

When on earth the Infant Jesus was hunted by King Herod, St. Joseph took Him and His mother, stealing away into the night. The devil hoped that through the tyrant King Herod, Jesus would be found and killed—putting a stop to God's plan for salvation. Even before Jesus was born, St. Joseph himself was tempted to abandon the Blessed Virgin and the coming Son of God, but Satan would be disappointed as Joseph would prove to be, by the grace of God, the most determined of men. St. Joseph was to become one of the devil's greatest adversaries — even to this day.

St. Joseph was rewarded for all that he had done on Earth for God's greater glory and has become a Prince in the Royal Court of Heaven as well as in the Holy Church on Earth. He has been granted the gifts of power and position and Satan knows this and loathes him for it. He reels with anger as he contemplates this man whom God has deigned to elevate as the noble Viceroy of Heaven, the Patron of the Church. Since the devil cannot destroy Jesus Christ, he tries to destroy the Church and those souls who are a part of it.

Pope Leo XIII, who knew the importance of St. Joseph and his position in Heaven, turned the Church, and the souls of the faithful, over to his care. The prayer he composed is thematically like the prayer addressed to St. Michael, stressing the invocation for protection. Pope Leo XIII ordered that this prayer be added to the conclusion of the Rosary, to be recited by the faithful.

To you, O Blessed Joseph, we come in our tribulations, and having asked the help of your most Holy Spouse, we confidently ask your patronage also. Through that sacred bond of charity which united you to the Immaculate Virgin Mother of God and through the fatherly love with which you embraced the Child Jesus, we humbly beg you to look graciously upon the beloved inheritance which Jesus Christ has purchased by His blood, and to aid us in our necessities with your power and strength. O, most provident guardian of the Holy Family, defend the chosen children of Jesus Christ. Most beloved father, dispel the evil of falsehood and sin.

Our most mighty protector graciously assist us from Heaven in our struggles with the powers of darkness. And just as you once saved the Child Jesus from mortal danger, so now defend God's Holy Church from the snares of Her enemies and from all adversity. Shield each one of us by your constant protection, so that, supported by your example and your aid, we may be able to live piously, to die holy, and to obtain eternal happiness in Heaven (Leo XIII, 1889).

Pope Leo XIII had given the command to invoke and venerate a man and an angel—both beloved by the Heavenly Father. St. Joseph and St. Michael the Archangel are given to us by God as militant saints who are entrusted with the honourable duty of defending the Mystical Body of Christ. Let the pleadings of this great Pontiff not be ignored, even today, but rather listened to.

ST. JOSEPH BLESSES THE WORLD

Thirty-three years after Pope Leo XIII's mystical experience, St. Joseph appeared at Fatima, Portugal on the very anniversary of the vision of Pope Leo, October 13, 1917. In this apparition, St. Joseph traced the Sign of The Cross with his right hand, blessing the estimated 70,000 people present, as if to say that he was still vigilant in his role as Patron of the Church and keeping watch over the faithful. He will not abandon God's Church, nor His people.

In the sky, we beheld St. Joseph with the Child Jesus, and our Lady robed in white with a blue mantle, beside the sun. St. Joseph and the Child Jesus appeared to bless the world, for they traced the Sign of the Cross with their hands (L. Santos, 2007, pg. 183).

THE CHURCH HONOURS ST. JOSEPH

Just as St. Joseph led his family into and out of exile, so too does he lead the Mystical Body of Christ, the Church, Who is currently experiencing hardships and trials as never seen before. Successive Popes since the time of Pius IX have continually exhorted the faithful to form a special devotion to St. Joseph the Patron of the Church and implore his aid for the Church. Among these pontiffs are Leo XIII, Benedict XV, Paul VI, Benedict XVI and Francis, to name a few, who have encouraged the faithful in this devotion.

> The Catholic Church rightly honours and venerates, with a feeling of deep reverence, the illustrious patriarch Blessed Joseph, now crowned with glory and honour in Heaven. On earth, Almighty God, in preference to all His saints, willed him to be the chaste and true spouse of the Immaculate Virgin Mary as well as the putative father of His Only-Begotten Son. He indeed enriched him and filled him to overflowing with entirely unique graces, enabling him to execute more faithfully the duties of so sublime a state (Pius IX, 1871).

> The Blessed Patriarch Joseph looks upon the multitude of Christians who make up the Church as confided especially to his trust – this limitless family spread over the earth, over which, because he is the spouse of Mary and the father of Jesus Christ, he holds, as it were, a paternal authority. It is, then, natural and worthy that as the Blessed Joseph ministered to all the needs of the family at Nazareth

and girt it about with his protection, he should now cover with the cloak of his heavenly patronage and defend the Church of Jesus Christ (Leo XIII, 1889).

We, full of confidence in the patronage of the one to whose provident supervision God was pleased to entrust the custody of His only-begotten Incarnate Son, and the Virgin Mother of God, earnestly exhort all the Bishops of the Catholic world that, in times so turbulent for Christianity, to induce the faithful to pray with greater commitment for the valuable help of St. Joseph. And since there are several ways approved by the Apostolic See with whom you can venerate the Holy Patriarch, especially every Wednesday throughout the year and month consecrated to him, We want, for every Bishop to heed these requests — that all these devotions, as much as possible, are practiced in every diocese (Benedict XV, 1920).

The Church invokes Saint Joseph as Her Patron and Protector through Her unshakable trust that he to whom Christ willed to confide the care and protection of His own frail human childhood, will continue from Heaven to perform his protective task to guide and defend the Mystical Body of Christ Himself, which is always weak, always under attack, always in a state of peril. We call upon St. Joseph for the world, trusting that the heart of the humble working man of Nazareth, now overflowing with immeasurable wisdom and power, still harbours and will always harbour a singular and precious fellow-feeling for the whole of mankind. So, may it be (Paul VI, 1969).

The life of Saint Joseph, lived in obedience to God's word, is an eloquent sign for all the disciples of Jesus who seek the unity of the Church. His example helps us to understand that it is only by complete submission to the will of God that we become effective workers in the service of His plan to gather together all mankind into one family, one assembly, one 'ecclesia' (Benedict XVI, 2009).

How does Joseph respond to his calling to be the protector of Mary, Jesus and the Church? By being constantly attentive to God, open to the signs of God's presence and receptive to God's plans, and not simply to his own. ... Joseph is a "protector" because he can hear God's voice and be guided by His will; and for this reason, he is more sensitive to the persons entrusted to his safekeeping. He can look at things realistically, he is in touch with his surroundings, and he can make truly wise decisions. In him, dear friends, we learn how to respond to God's call, readily and willingly, but we also see the core of the Christian vocation, which is Christ! Let us protect Christ in our lives, so that we can protect others, so that we can protect creation (Francis, 2013)!

CONSECRATION OF THE VATICAN CITY STATE

As a further show of the papacy's fidelity to St. Joseph, His Holiness Pope Francis has consecrated the Vatican City State to the protection of both St. Michael the Archangel and St. Joseph, on July 5, 2014, reminding the faithful the importance of their mission:

Michael is the champion of the primacy of God, of His transcendence and power. Michael struggles to restore divine justice and defends the people of God from His enemies, above all from the enemy par excellence, the devil. And St. Michael wins because in him, there is his God who acts. ... Though the devil always tries to disfigure the face of the Archangel and that of humanity, God is stronger; it is His victory and His salvation that is offered to all men. ... In consecrating the Vatican City State to St. Michael, the Archangel, I ask him to defend us from the evil one and banish him.

We also consecrate Vatican City State to St. Joseph, guardian of Jesus, the guardian of the Holy Family. May his presence make us stronger and more courageous in making space for God in our lives to always defeat evil with good. We ask him to protect us, take care of us, so that a life of grace grows stronger in each of us every day (Francis, 2014).

CHAPTER 5: PATRON AGAINST POLITICAL EVIL

This chapter speaks of the entrustment of the Church's war against Socialism and Communism to the hands of St. Joseph.

PATRON AGAINST COMMUNISM AND SOCIALISM

The twentieth century saw the rise of Socialism and Communism – enemies of the Church and the Christian worker. Knowing full well the threat of these powers, a succession of Pontiffs saw fit to warn the faithful and to entrust them to the care of St. Joseph.

On July 25, 1920 Pope Benedict XV, known as the "Pope of Peace" during World War I, issued the motu proprio "Bonum Sane" in which he warned the faithful of Socialism and World Government, while also entrusting them to the care of St. Joseph:

> We now see, with true sorrow, that society is now much more depraved and corrupt than before, and that the so-called *"social question"* has been aggravating to such an extent as to create the threat of irreparable ruin. ... This World Government will no longer acknowledge the authority of the father over his children, or of the public power over the citizens, or of God over human society. All things will, if implemented, lead to terrible social convulsions, like those which are already happening ... We, therefore, concerned most of all by the course of these events ... remind those on Our side, who earn their bread by their work, to save them from Socialism, the sworn enemy of Christian principles, that with great solicitude We recommend them to St. Joseph, to follow him as their guide and to receive the special honour of his heavenly patronage (Benedict XV, 1920).

Pope Pius XI, who succeeded Benedict XV, also saw the growing threat against the Church. In his 1937 encyclical "Divini Redemptoris" he decided to explicitly entrust the cause against Communism to St. Joseph:

> To hasten the advent of that "peace of Christ in the kingdom of Christ" so ardently desired by all, We entrust the vast campaign of the Church against world Communism under the standard of St. Joseph, Her mighty Protector. He belongs to the working-class, and he bore the burdens of poverty for himself and the Holy Family, whose tender and vigilant head he was. To him was entrusted the Divine Child when Herod loosed his assassins against Him. In a life of faithful performance of everyday duties, he left an example for all those who must gain their bread by the toil of their hands. He won for himself the title of "The Just," serving thus as a living model of that Christian justice which should reign in social life (Pius XI, 1937).

In 1955 the successor to Pius XI, Venerable Pope Pius XII, established the Feast Day of "St. Joseph the Worker" to be celebrated annually on May 1. This date was specifically chosen to counteract the predominantly Socialist and Communist holiday "International Workers' Day," also known as "May Day." In an address on May 1, 1955, Pius XII encouraged labourers to look to St. Joseph as their model and to ask for his intercession in their work:

> St. Joseph is the best protector to help you in your life, to penetrate the spirit of the Gospel. Indeed, from the Heart of the God-Man, Saviour of the world, this

spirit is infused in you and in all men, but it is certain that there was no worker's spirit so perfectly and deeply penetrated as the putative father of Jesus, who lived with Him in the closest intimacy and community of family and work. So, if you want to be close to Christ, I repeat to you "Ite ad Ioseph": Go to Joseph (Pius XII, 1955).

CHAPTER 6: IN GOD'S TIME

This chapter speaks of the emergence of St. Joseph into full view of the faithful.

... one day with the Lord is as a thousand years, and
a thousand years is as one day (2 Peter 8 ESV).

For centuries St. Joseph has remained hidden in the background of the greater picture, only periodically emerging when he was needed. But everything is done in God's time and ultimately His Divine Will is accomplished exactly when He sees fit. One could say that the first millennium was reserved for the sole exploration of who Jesus Christ was and continues to be for His followers. It was a time for discernment and meditation on the Word of God, Who came to save humanity from sin so that eternal life may be given. The Church was given insights into the life, death, and resurrection of Jesus Christ to understand God's plan for mankind and the realization of the person of God in Him, as the second person of the Most Holy Trinity, defined as truth. Jesus is the New Adam who came to fulfill what was written in the books of the Prophets and to lead His people into new life. He gave the Church the gift of the Holy Spirit to continue His saving work on earth, to sustain His Mystical Body, the Church.

For as by the disobedience of one man, many were
made sinners; so also, by the obedience of one, many
shall be made just (Romans 5:19 DRV).

THE BLESSED VIRGIN MARY

The next millennium would be focused on knowing Christ more intimately through those closest to Him. Who better to show the Church how to love Jesus than His own mother, the Blessed Virgin Mary? These years were given to teach how to emulate her, and to be led by her example of humility, in true love for

Christ. She is not a stumbling block on the way to Christ—she leads straight to Him. Our Lady guides the faithful to her dearly beloved Son, who is always ready to receive sinners, especially from His mother's hands. Let it be known that Jesus is the only mediator between God the Father and man. Since Jesus is the only one begotten of the Father as both God and man, Mary's role is to draw His people to closer to union with Him, for she is His greatest disciple. Her intercessory role echoes that of Queen Esther who pleaded before the king for her people in the Old Testament. In the Gospel of St. Luke, someone from the crowd praises Mary for giving birth to Jesus, but Jesus says instead that she is blessed because she has heard the Word of God and has held true to it. Jesus says this to show that anyone among them may be called "blessed", but only in holding steadfast to the Word of God as she does.

> Blessed is the womb that bore You, and the breasts that nursed You!" But (Jesus said) "Blessed rather are those who hear the Word of God and obey it (Luke 11:27-28 NRSV)."

ENTER ST. JOSEPH

The current millennium seems to be open to St. Joseph, the Guardian of the Redeemer, who up until recently was hidden, in a way. The faithful are discovering his role not only within the pious walls of the Church, but also in their daily lives. Why is this important? Why does one need Joseph?

Joseph has emerged at this critical time in history because now more than ever a human father is needed, a noble model of manhood for these troublesome times, as there is a war currently being waged on manhood.

Fathers, or "breeders" (as some people dare to label heterosexual men, quite derogatorily,) are shamed from exercising any rights over their children. It is the children who are encouraged to make their own decisions, even those of an extremely serious, adult nature (or unnatural nature), such as the now popular theme of changing sexes. The "breeders" no longer have a say in what is best for their children. Their sole purpose is to bring the child into the world and be as accommodating as possible to their whims and ideas – regardless of health, safety, or salvific risks.

There is a shaming of parenthood when one tries to make important decisions for children, when one tries to discipline them, or even in giving them spiritual formation. The common phrase from parents these days is "I'll let my child decide what they want". Fathers no longer have the rights accorded to him by God as they have been taken away by the world. God is no longer the judge of humanity but, rather, the ungodly public is. Pope Benedict XV warned us about this sort of thing one hundred years ago! And who did the Pontiff give the faithful as a model and protector for those evil times? St. Joseph. How much more do we need him now, in this diabolical 21st century. The Pope's words are so in tune with our present state that he could easily have uttered them this morning:

> We now see, with true sorrow, that society is now much more depraved and corrupt than before, … This World Government will no longer acknowledge the authority of the father over his children, or of the public power over the citizens, or of God over human society. We, therefore, concerned most of all by the course of these events … recommend the faithful to St. Joseph, to follow him as their guide and to receive the special honour of his heavenly patronage (Benedict XV, 1920).

ST. JOSEPH AND FATHERHOOD

St. Joseph has raised the bar for fathers to come. The Heavenly Father has given mankind a completely human father as a pattern for what true paternity is. Joseph is God's model of real fatherhood, Mary is the perfect image of motherhood, and Christ is the ideal of true and perfect sonship and brotherhood. Because of this earthly trinity, there is the perfect family blueprint for the most imperfect of times. St. Joseph teaches, by his life, that fatherhood goes beyond genetics, and now, more than ever, he is a role model for both biological and adoptive parents. Though Christ is not of his flesh, Joseph accepts Him as his own Son as He grows within the sanctuary of Mary's womb.

From the moment that Jesus was conceived by the Holy Spirit, He took on the human nature of His chosen father, Joseph, and the flesh and blood of Mary. When St. Joseph accepted his role of father, he became the Patron of Fatherhood and the Unborn, the loving guardian of the helpless and innocent. Just as he loved the unborn Redeemer while still in His mother's womb, so too does he love all the children of this world. And just as he wept for the children who were massacred by King Herod, so too does he now weep for those who are aborted every day, all around the world.

> Behold, sons are a gift from the Lord; the fruit of the womb is a reward (Psalm 127:3 NRSV).

> Truly You have formed my inmost being; You knit me in my mother's womb. I praise You, so wonderfully you made me; wonderful are Your works! My very self You knew (Psalm 139:13-15 NASB).

Joseph is also a model for those men who are afraid or hesitant to take on the responsibility of raising a child. So many young men are faced with the news that their wife or girlfriend is pregnant. A flood of panic overtakes many of them, especially those who are unmarried, and in their despair, they run away from their responsibilities, abandoning mother and child. It is this act of abandonment that leads many children to be aborted by their mothers, not out of malice but out of fear. Who better to be a guide for these men than St. Joseph? St. Joseph was faced with the same situation as these men and almost resorted to sending his beloved, and the child within her, away. In the end, though, he did the right thing and took his rightful place as husband and father. He knows what it was like to almost lose his wife and son, and if men would only look to him, chosen by the Eternal Father, they would know that he understands how they feel. He was confused, scared, and full of anxiety, but the love of a father for his son outweighs these frustrations. He was truly predestined above all other men to take on the role of Father of the Redeemer and Spouse of the Blessed Virgin.

> Be on the alert, stand firm in the faith, act like men, be strong. Let all that you do be done in love (1 Corinthians 16:13-14 NASB).

Who protected the unborn child within Mary's womb? Joseph, by the grace of God. Who made sacrifices for his family and put their needs above his own? Joseph. Now more than ever, the "just man" is needed to lead by example, how to live in the truth. These excerpts from the Proverbs of Solomon describe the just man, which well represent St. Joseph and the men we need today.

> The blessing of the Lord is upon the head of the just ... He that walketh sincerely, walketh confidently ... The work of the just is unto life ... The expectation of the just is joy ... The strength of the upright is the way of the Lord ... Where pride is, there also shall be

179

reproach: but where humility is, there also is wisdom. The simplicity of the just shall guide them. The justice of the upright shall make his way prosperous ... The just is delivered out of distress ... The fruit of the just man is a tree of life: and he that gaineth souls is wise (Proverbs 10, 11 DRV).

On March 19, 2009, while visiting Yaoundé, Cameroon, Pope Benedict XVI recommended that fathers look to St. Joseph as a model of true fatherhood and husbandry:

> I wish to extend a word of encouragement to fathers so that they may take Saint Joseph as their model. He who kept watch over the Son of Man can teach them the deepest meaning of their own fatherhood. In the same way, each father receives his children from God, and they are created in God's own image and likeness. Saint Joseph was the spouse of Mary. In the same way, each father sees himself entrusted with the mystery of womanhood through his own wife. Dear fathers, like Saint Joseph, respect and love your spouse; and by your love and your wise presence, lead your children to God where they must be (Benedict XVI, 2009).

PART FOUR: APPARITIONS OF ST. JOSEPH

You will know them by their fruits. ... every good tree bears good fruit, but the bad tree bears bad fruit. A good tree cannot bear bad fruit; nor can a bad tree bear good fruit. ... Thus, you will know them by their fruits (Matthew 7:16-20 NRSV).

As far as visitations or apparitions of St. Joseph are concerned, they are far and few between – especially when compared to those of Christ or the Blessed Virgin Mary. When it comes to discerning these apparitions, the Church performs a lengthy and exhaustive investigation, taking great pains to determine the authenticity of alleged apparitions. The findings are then categorized as:

Worthy of Belief (meaning this comes from God), Not Worthy of Belief (meaning this is imagined or from the devil), Nothing Contrary to the Faith (undecided on authenticity, but note that there is nothing contrary to the faith, further investigation may be required).

Regarding apparitions, the faithful must always await the approval of Holy Mother Church before fully accepting them. In some cases, the local Bishop will approve the apparitions in an official document or will approve the promotion of messages of the apparitions with an Imprimatur or Nihil Obstat and the faithful are permitted to practice devotions associated with the visions. The belief in apparitions is not binding on the faithful.

HELFTA, GERMANY – 13th CENTURY
Witness: St. Gertrude the Great

St. Gertrude of Helfta was a scholarly sister of the Benedictine Order who was given to mystical experiences and ecstasies. She received visions and locutions from our Lord Jesus, as well as the saints, and was a great lover of the Souls of Purgatory. She is the only female saint to possess the title "the

Great," given to her by Pope Benedict XIV. She relates a vision she had of St. Joseph:

"On the Feast of the Annunciation, I saw Heaven opened and St. Joseph sitting upon a magnificent throne. I felt myself wonderfully affected when, each time his name was mentioned, all the Saints made a profound inclination toward him, showing by the serenity and sweetness of their looks that they rejoiced with him on account of his exalted dignity."

COAST OF FLANDERS – 16th Century
Witnesses: Two Unnamed Franciscan Fathers

In the 16th Century there arose a devotion called "The Seven Our Fathers of Saint Joseph", which would later be known as "The Seven Sorrows and Joys". The devotion as it appears today is credited to Blessed Gennaro Sarnelli (1702-1744). Below is related the brief story of how this devotion came to be requested by St. Joseph himself:

There were once two priests of the Franciscan order who were sailing along the coast of Flanders. A terrible tempest arose, sinking the ship along with 300 passengers. The two Fathers grabbed hold of a nearby plank, embracing it for dear life, as they were tossed about in the violent waves. All the while the two men had recourse to St. Joseph, praying and begging for his assistance, to save them in the name of God from their most helpless and dire situation.

On the third day someone came to their aid, appearing as a most radiant man, encouraging them to have faith and to continue to confide in St. Joseph. The mysterious man safely conducted them into a harbor much to the happiness and relief of the two priests. Upon arriving safely, they thanked him repeatedly and asked for the name of the man who had just saved their lives. The man revealed to them that he was none other than St. Joseph — the one to whom they had prayed all this time.

The two priests wanting to extend some form of honour or respect to the Saint for all that he had done for them, asked what they could do to show their gratitude. St. Joseph told them to honour him thusly: to recite daily the "Our Father" and "Hail Mary" seven times while meditating on his seven sorrows and seven joys. After advising them, he disappeared as mysteriously as he had come.

THE SEVEN SORROWS & JOYS OF ST. JOSEPH

A just man shall fall seven times and shall rise again.
– Proverbs 24:16

I – The Despair of St. Joseph (St. Matthew 1:19)
The Annunciation to St. Joseph (St. Matthew 1:20-24)

II – The Poverty of Jesus' Birth (St. Luke 2:7)
The Birth of the Saviour of Mankind (St. Luke 2:10-19)

III – The Circumcision of Jesus (St. Luke 2:21)
The Holy Name of Jesus (St. Matthew 1:25)
IV – Simeon's Prophecy (St. Luke 2:34, 35)
The Salvation of Mankind (St. Luke 2:29-33)

V – The Flight into Egypt (St. Matthew 2:13-14)
The Toppling of the Idols (Isaiah 19:1)

VI – The Perilous Return from Exile (St. Matthew 2:19-22)
Family Life at Nazareth (St. Luke 2:51-52)

VII – The Loss of Jesus in Jerusalem (St. Luke 2:42-45)
The Finding of Jesus in the Temple (St. Luke 2:46-49)

QUEBEC, CANADA (NEW FRANCE) – 17th CENTURY
Witness: Blessed Catherine de St. Augustine

Blessed Catherine de St. Augustine is honoured as one of the six founders of the Catholic Church in Canada. Upon her arrival in New France (Quebec, Canada) in 1648, Blessed Catherine ministered to the sick of both the Aboriginal and European populations. She was known to have visions of our Lord, the saints and of future events in Canada. She recorded her vision of St. Joseph:

"I saw a very august procession of blessed souls ... John the Baptist was at the head and carried a white banner, white as snow, on which was written in large red characters these words: Ecce Agnus Dei, ecce qui tollit peccata mundi. This procession seemed to rise in the air ... St. Joseph was the closest at the entrance of the eternal gates, and it was he, it seemed to me, who spoke first to the Most August Trinity; and addressing himself to the person of God the Father, after the holy souls were put into their appointed place, said to Him in a language of the blessed:

'This talent has profited so much that not only do I return it to You doubled, but You see this multitude that it has acquired; I return all to You and offer it to You.'

The Eternal Father then not only set him over a great many people, but even said to him: "Faithful servant! Since you were the steward of My house on earth, I want you to command here and to have power." The Son Himself gave him power over Him, all King of glory that He was, and wanted him to have the honour of commanding Him.

Then, hence, turning to St. Joseph, I said to him: "Great saint, I am one of yours; ask of the King of glory that through all eternity I not be separated from His love. He will refuse you nothing."

AGREDA, SPAIN – 17th Century
Witness: Venerable María de Jesús

Throughout the 17th century, Franciscan Abbess María de Jesús received revelations from the Blessed Virgin Mary, telling her life story, which included our Lord Jesus Christ and St. Joseph. She compiled these revelations in her monumental work *Mystical City of God*. Below are the words from Our Lady to María de Jesús concerning St. Joseph's intercession:

"My daughter, though you have described my spouse, St. Joseph, as the most noble among the princes and saints of the heavenly Jerusalem; you cannot properly manifest his eminent sanctity, nor can any of the mortals know it fully before they arrive at the vision of the Divinity. Then all of them will be filled with wonder

187

and praise as the Lord will make them capable of understanding this sacrament. On the last day, when all men shall be judged, the damned will bitterly bewail their sins, which prevented them from appreciating this powerful means of their salvation, and availing themselves, as they easily could have, of St. Joseph the intercessor, to gain the friendship of the just Judge.

The whole human race has much undervalued the privileges and prerogatives conceded to my Blessed Spouse Joseph and they do not know what his intercession with God can do. I assure you, my dearest, that he is one of the greatly favoured personages in the divine presence and has immense power to stay the arms of divine vengeance.

I desire that from now on, during the rest of your mortal life, you advance in devotion and in heartfelt love toward my Spouse, and that you bless the Lord for having favoured him with such high privileges and for having rejoiced me so much in the knowledge of all his excellences. In all your necessities, you must avail yourself of his intercession. You should induce many to venerate him and see that your own religious sisters distinguish themselves in their devotion to him. That which my spouse asks of the Lord in Heaven is granted upon the earth and on his intercession depend many and extraordinary favours for men, if they do not make themselves unworthy of receiving them. All these privileges were to be a reward for the amiable perfection of this wonderful Saint and for his great virtues; for divine clemency is favourably drawn forth by them and looks upon Saint Joseph with generous liberality, ready to shower down its marvelous mercies upon all those who avail themselves of his intercession."

COTIGNAC, FRANCE – 1660
Witness: Gaspard Ricard

On June 7th of 1660 a shepherd of 22 years of age, Gaspard Ricard, was herding his sheep to the east side of Mount Bessillon. At roughly 1pm the heat grew stronger and harder to bear. Very tired and thirsty, he decided to lay upon the rocky ground for a rest when out of nowhere a tall man stood next to him and pointed to a nearby rock saying:

"I am Joseph, lift the rock and you will drink."

The startled young man saw that the large rock looked heavy and stated that it would take about eight men to move it. He asked how he would be able to do this alone as there were no other men around besides him. St. Joseph reiterated his instruction to lift the rock. Gaspard obeyed and, finding himself able to move the rock, found fresh water flowing from underneath. He began to drink excitedly and looking up he found that St. Joseph had disappeared. With haste, he ran into town exclaiming this news to the villagers and within three hours the small spring of water had now become a fountain of overabundant water.

As a result of this occurrence King Louis XIV (1638-1715) decreed that day, June 7th, to be a holiday and, after making his own pilgrimage to this place, he consecrated France – as well as himself – to St. Joseph. These waters which sprang forth in

Cotignac, France, would become a sign of hope for many people as the waters were found to have curative properties for both the body and the soul. There now stands at that place a sanctuary dedicated to the honour of St. Joseph. One of the documented

miracles that took place was recorded in 1662 by a priest who had gone there the previous year:

"The waters of St. Joseph bring miracles. Since I returned, a man whom we know from Avignon, born lame, went to the spring and came back cured, having left his crutches there. Everyone drinks and carries away the water." – Father Allard of the Oratory, 1662

KNOCK, IRELAND – 1879

Witnesses: Dominick Byrne Sr, Dominick Byrne Jr., Margaret Byrne, Mary Byrne, Mrs. Margaret Byrne, Patrick Byrne, Judith Campbell, John Curry, John Durkan, Mrs. Flatley, Patrick Hill, Mary McLoughlin, Catherine Murray, Bridget Trench, and Patrick Walsh

At 8pm on August 21st 1879, a diverse group of fifteen people including men, women and children, beheld a silent vision of the Blessed Virgin Mary with hands and eyes raised toward Heaven and wearing a crown upon her head, St. Joseph robed in white with hands joined and head bowed, and St. John the Evangelist wearing a Bishop's mitre and holding a large Bible. They appeared at the south gable of the Knock Parish Church in a blaze of glorious light. Behind them, to the left of St. John, was a simple altar, with a Lamb (symbol of Jesus Christ, the Lamb of God) standing on it. Adoring at the altar was a group of angels.

St. Joseph appeared to be close to middle-age with hints of gray in his hair. He was clothed in white robes, standing bare foot at the Virgin Mary's right-hand side. His head was inclined forward and appeared to be paying his respects to his Blessed Spouse, and adoring the Lamb on the altar, his hands joined in prayer. He was the figure of humility and of a gentle disposition, in contemplation of the Holy Virgin and the Lamb of God. He is showing the people to have reverence for the Mass and to honour the Mother of God. The faithful must be like St. Joseph in his humility and prayerfulness, setting aside trials and distractions to spend more time in quiet contemplation of God and His works. Below are related some of the eye-witness accounts:

Mary Byrne: I beheld, standing out from the gable, three figures which appeared to be that of the Blessed Virgin, St. Joseph and St. John ... They stood a little distance out from the gable wall, and, as well as I could judge a foot and a half or two feet from the ground. The Virgin stood erect, with eyes raised to Heaven ... In the figure of St. Joseph, the head was slightly bent, and inclined towards the Blessed Virgin, as if paying her respect. ... The third

figure appeared to be that of St. John the Evangelist. ... Above the altar and resting on it, was a lamb, standing with the face towards St. John, thus fronting the western sky. On the body of the lamb and around it, I saw golden stars.

Patrick Hill: I saw St. Joseph to the Blessed Virgin's right hand; his head was bent, from the shoulders, forward; he appeared to be paying his respects; I noticed his whiskers; they appeared slightly grey; I saw the feet of St. Joseph, too. His hands were joined like a person at prayer ... For the space of an hour and a half we were under the pouring rain; at this time, I was very wet; I noticed that the rain did not wet the figures which appeared before me, although I was wet myself.

Dominick Byrne: I beheld the three figures: The Blessed Virgin, St. Joseph, and St. John. The eyes of the images could be seen; they did not speak. I was filled with wonder at the sight I saw; I was so affected that I shed tears.

FATIMA, PORTUGAL – 1917
Witnesses: St. Jacinta Marto, St. Francisco Marto and Servant of God Lucia dos Santos

From May to October 1917 three shepherd children beheld apparitions of the Blessed Virgin Mary atop a small holm-oak tree. During these visions, the seers were given secrets, were instructed to pray the Rosary, and told to offer penance for the conversion of sinners. In the September apparition, our Lady told them:

"Continue to pray the Rosary in order to obtain the end of the war. In October St. Joseph will appear with the Child Jesus in order to bless the world. God is satisfied with your sacrifices..."

On October 13th it is estimated that over 70,000 people gathered around the site of the apparitions. After our Lady appeared to the

three children, thousands of people from different walks of life (including atheists who had gone to mock the children) witnessed what is now famously known as "The Miracle of the Sun." During the miracle, the three shepherd children were witnessing what the Virgin had promised them in September. Servant of God Lucia dos Santos recounts what they saw:

"Our Lady having disappeared in the immensity of the firmament, we saw, beside the sun St. Joseph with the Child Jesus (both to the left of the sun), and our Lady (on the right side of it), clothed in white with a blue mantle. St. Joseph and the Child Jesus wore red. Jesus appeared to be two years of age. St. Joseph appeared to bless the world, for he traced the Sign of the Cross with his hand."

Here is St. Joseph, no words are spoken by him, but his actions speak. St. Joseph, holding his Son Jesus, blesses the world by tracing the Sign of the Cross with his hand. This is a powerful statement regarding his place as head of the Holy Family as well as his position in the Church. He holds Christ in his arms, making a statement about true fatherhood: "Fathers, love your children, take your place at the head of the family and protect those entrusted to your care." The act of St. Joseph blessing the crowds shows his power in the Church, as intercessor and Patron of the Universal Church, as proclaimed in 1870 by Pope Pius IX.

KRAKOW, POLAND: 1936 – 1937
Witness: St. Faustina Kowalska

St. Faustina Kowalska is best known for making the message of "Divine Mercy" known to the world – having received messages and visions of our Lord Jesus and the

Blessed Virgin Mary. A little-known fact, St. Faustina was also blessed to behold St. Joseph on some rare occasions but only once did he speak to her. Related here are her diary entries in which St. Faustina mentions seeing St. Joseph, accompanied with

Jesus and Mary, and the one time he spoke to her.

February 2, 1936: (Diary Entry 608) When Mass began, a strange silence and joy filled my heart. Just then, I saw Our Lady with the Infant Jesus, and the holy man St. Joseph standing behind them. The most holy Mother said to me: "Take my dearest Treasure ..." and she handed me the Infant Jesus. When I took the Infant Jesus in my arms, the Mother of God and St. Joseph disappeared. I was left alone with the Infant Jesus.

December 25, 1936: (Diary Entry 846) During Midnight Mass, God's presence pierced me through and through. A moment before the Elevation (of the Host) I saw the Mother of God, the Infant Jesus, and the good man St. Joseph.

July 30, 1937: (Diary Entry 1203) St. Joseph urged me to have a constant devotion to him. He himself told me to recite these prayers: Our Father, Hail Mary, Glory Be, and the Memorare to St. Joseph, once every day. He looked at me with great kindness and gave me to know how much he is supporting this work (of mercy). He has promised me his special help and protection. I recite the requested prayers every day and feel his special protection.

December 25, 1937: (Diary Entry 1442) When I arrived at Midnight Mass, from the very beginning I steeped myself in deep recollection, during which time I saw the stable of Bethlehem filled with great radiance. The Blessed Virgin, all lost in the deepest of love, was wrapping Jesus in swaddling clothes, but St. Joseph was still asleep. Only after the Mother of God put Jesus in the manger, did the light of God awaken Joseph, who was also praying. But after a while, I was left alone with the Infant Jesus who stretched out His little hands to me, and I understood that I was to take Him in my arms. Jesus pressed His head against my heart and gave me to know, by His profound gaze, how good He found it to be next to my heart. At that moment Jesus disappeared and the bell was ringing for Holy Communion.

INDIANA, USA – 1956 & 1958
Witness: Sister Mary Ephrem Neuzil

Beginning in 1938, Washington, DC, USA, a sister of the Congregation of the Precious Blood, Sister Mary Ephrem, began receiving locutions from Christ. These inner locutions were later followed by apparitions of the Archangels Michael and Gabriel. On September 25, 1956, while stationed in Rome City, Indiana, the Blessed Virgin Mary, to be known as "Our Lady of America", began appearing to her. The main theme of the apparitions was the call to purity and conversion of the United States and for the sanctification of the family. While our Lady continued to appear to Sister Mary Ephrem for the next few years, it was in October of 1956 that she received an inner locution from St. Joseph, followed by his  apparitions in 1958 in which he spoke of his spiritual fatherhood, his protection of the Catholic Church and requested devotion to his Most Pure Heart.

It is known that Archbishop Paul F. Leilbold, spiritual director of Sister Mary Ephrem, was a supporter of the apparitions, granting the Imprimatur to the messages and having medals struck per the instructions of Our Lady of America. More recently, in a letter dated May 31, 2007, Archbishop Raymond L. Burke (now Cardinal Burke) states:

"What can be concluded canonically is that the devotion was both approved by Archbishop Leibold and, what is more, was actively promoted by him. In addition, over the years, other Bishops have approved the devotion and have participated in public devotion to the Mother of God, under the title of 'Our Lady of America'."

October 1956: In early October 1956, about a week after our Lady's first appearance, St. Joseph, though I did not see him at this time, spoke to me the following words:

"It is true, my daughter, that immediately after my conception I was, through the future merits of Jesus and because of my exceptional role of future Virgin-Father, cleansed from the stain of original sin. I was from that moment confirmed in grace and never had the slightest stain on my soul. This is my unique privilege among men.

My Pure Heart was also from the first moment of existence inflamed with love for God. Immediately, at the moment when my soul was cleansed from original sin, grace was infused into it in such abundance that, excluding my holy spouse, I surpassed the holiness of the highest angel in the angelic choir. My Heart suffered with the Hearts of Jesus and Mary. Mine was a silent suffering, for it was my special vocation to hide and shield, as long as God willed, the Virgin Mother and Son from the malice and hatred of men.

The most painful of my sorrows was that I knew beforehand of their passion yet would not be there to console them. Their future suffering was ever present to me and became my daily cross, so I became, in union with my holy spouse, co-redemptor of humanity. Through compassion for the sufferings of Jesus and Mary I co-operated, as no other, in the salvation of the world."

March 11, 1958: Our Lady said to me: "St. Joseph will come. Prepare yourself well. There will be a special message. My holy spouse has an important part to play in bringing peace to the world."

March 18, 1958: St. Joseph came as was promised, and these are the words he spoke at this time: "Kneel, my daughter, for what you will hear and what you will write will bring countless souls to a new way of life. Through you, small one, the Trinity desires to make known to souls Its desire to be adored, honoured, and loved within the kingdom, the interior kingdom of their hearts.

I bring to souls the purity of my life and the obedience that crowned it. All fatherhood is blessed in me whom the Eternal Father chose as His representative on earth, the Virgin-Father of His own Divine Son. Through me the Heavenly Father has blessed all fatherhood, and through me He continues and will continue to do so till the end of time.

My spiritual fatherhood extends to all God's children, and together with my Virgin Spouse I watch over them with great love and solicitude. Fathers must come to me, small one, to learn obedience to authority: to the Church always, as the mouthpiece of God, to the laws of the country in which they live, insofar as these do not go against God and their neighbor. Mine was perfect obedience to the Divine Will, as it was shown and made known to me by the Jewish Law and religion. To be careless in this is most displeasing to God and will be severely punished in the next world.

Let fathers also imitate my great purity of life and the deep respect I held for my Immaculate Spouse. Let them be an example to their children and fellow men, never willfully doing anything that would cause scandal among God's people. Fatherhood is from God, and it must take once again its rightful place among men."

As St. Joseph ceased speaking, I saw his Most Pure Heart:

The Most Pure Heart of St. Joseph seemed to be lying on a cross which was of brown colour. It appeared to me that at the top of the Heart, in the midst of the flames pouring out, was a pure white lily. Then I heard these words: "Behold this Pure Heart so pleasing to Him who made it."

St. Joseph then continued: "The cross, my little one, upon which my Heart rests is the cross of the Passion, which was ever present before me, causing me intense suffering. I desire souls to come to my Heart that they may learn true union with the Divine Will. It is enough, my child; I will come again tomorrow. Then I will make known to you how God wishes me to be honoured in union with Jesus and Mary to obtain peace among men and nations. Good night, my little one."

March 19, 1958: On the evening of the next day, March 19, 1958, St. Joseph again appeared to me as he had promised and addressed me in these words:

"My child, I desire a day to be set aside to honour my fatherhood. The privilege of being chosen by God to be the Virgin-Father of His Son was mine alone, and no honour, excluding that bestowed upon my Holy Spouse, was ever, or will ever, be as sublime or as high as this. The Holy Trinity desires thus to honour me that in my unique fatherhood all fatherhood might be blessed.

Dear child, I was king in the little home of Nazareth, for I sheltered within it the Prince of Peace and the Queen of Heaven. To me they looked for protection and sustenance, and I did not fail them. I received from them the deepest love and reverence, for in me they saw Him Whose place I took over them. So, the head of the family must be loved, obeyed, and respected, and in return be a true father and protector to those under his care. In honouring in a special way my fatherhood, you also honour Jesus and Mary. The Divine Trinity has placed into our keeping the peace of the world. The imitation of the Holy Family, my child, of the virtues we practiced in our little home at Nazareth is the way for all souls to that peace which comes from God alone and which none other can give."

Then suddenly, as he ceased speaking, I was favoured with a unique and marvelous vision of the glorious St. Joseph:

St. Joseph seemed suspended, as it were, a short distance above what had the appearance of a large globe with clouds moving about it. His head was slightly raised, the eyes gazing upward as if in ecstasy. The hands were in a position similar to that of the priest during the celebration of Holy Mass, only they extended upward somewhat. The colour of his hair, as also of his rather small and slightly forked beard, seemed a very dark brown. His eyes resembled in colour the hair and beard.

He was clothed in a white robe that reached to his ankles. Over this he wore a sort of cloak which did not come together at the throat but covering the shoulders and draped gracefully over each arm, reached to the hem of the robe. The cloak at times had, or seemed to have, the appearance of a brown, sometimes a purple, hue, or perhaps a slight blending of the two. The belt about his waist was of a gold colour, as were his sandals.

His appearance, though quite youthful, gave at the same time the impression of rare maturity combined with great strength. He seemed a bit taller than medium height. The lines of his face appeared strong and purposeful, softened somewhat by a gentle serenity. I also saw his most Pure Heart at this time.

Moreover, I saw the Holy Spirit in the form of a dove hovering above his head. Standing sideways, facing each other, were two angels, one on the right, the other on the left. Each carried what appeared to be a small pillow in a satin covering, the pillow on the right bearing a gold crown, the one on the left, a gold sceptre. The angels were all white, ever their faces and hair. It was a beautiful whiteness that reminded me of the stainlessness of Heaven.

Then I heard these words: "Thus, should he be honoured whom the King desires to honour."

When the vision ended, St. Joseph before taking leave spoke to me in the following manner: "The Holy Father need have no fear, for I have been appointed his special protector. As God chose me to be the special guardian of His Son, so has He chosen me as the special guardian of him who in Christ's Name is head of the Mystical Body of that same Son on earth.

My special protection of the Holy Father and the Church should be made known to him. God wishes to make this known to him that he may receive thereby renewed consolation and encouragement. During the war, little daughter, it was I who saved him from death at the hands of his enemies*. Continually I watch over him and the Church, and I desire this to be acknowledged for the greater glory of God and the good of souls.

Lovely child, precious to the heart of your spiritual father, I will come again on the last Sunday of this month. Jesus and Mary will come also in a special visit. Receive my blessing."

As I knelt down to receive it, I felt his hands on my head and heard the words: "May Jesus and Mary, through my hands, bestow upon you eternal peace."

It had been revealed at the Nuremberg Trials (November 1945 – October 1946) that, in 1943, a plot was devised by Hitler to kidnap and possibly murder Pope Pius XII and members of the Roman Curia.

March 30, 1958: As he had promised, St. Joseph came again – accompanied by Jesus and Mary. His requests were similar to those of our Lady and the First Saturday Devotion. The Sacred Hearts of Jesus, Mary, and Joseph have been chosen by the Most Holy Trinity to bring peace to the world; hence, their request for special love and honour, also reparation and imitation.

"I am the protector of the Church and the home, as I was the protector of Christ and His Mother while I lived upon earth. Jesus and Mary desire that my Pure Heart, so long hidden and unknown, be now honoured in a special way. Let my children honour my Most Pure Heart in a special manner on the First Wednesday of the month by reciting the Joyful Mysteries of the Rosary in memory of my life with Jesus and Mary and the love I bore them, the sorrow I suffered with them.

Let them receive Holy Communion in union with the love with which I received the Saviour for the first time and each time I held Him in my arms. Those who honour me in this way will be consoled by my presence at their death, and I will conduct them safely into the presence of Jesus and Mary. I will come again, little child of my Most Pure Heart. Until then, continue in patience and humility, which is so pleasing to God."

ITAPIRANGA, BRAZIL
1996 – Present
Witness: Edson Glauber

Since May 2, 1994, the Blessed Virgin Mary under the title of "Queen of the

Rosary and of Peace", our Lord Jesus Christ, and St. Joseph, are said to have been appearing regularly in Itapiranga, Brazil. The apparitions, though thematically like the apparitions at Fatima, Portugal – a call to prayer and conversion, are unique in that we are given recurring visits from St. Joseph. Beginning in 1996 St. Joseph himself began appearing, recommending devotion to his Most Chaste Heart to obtain graces for the Church and for mankind. The messages contained herein pertain to St. Joseph specifically.

These apparitions were approved by the local Bishop, Dom Carillo Gritti on January 31, 2010, and the construction of a shrine was begun. However, after Bishop Carillo's death in 2016, the Diocesan Administrator has advised the Congregation for the Doctrine of the Faith to withdraw approval. This apparition is currently under reinvestigation. Apparitions of St. Joseph leading up to the initial approval are listed here for your discernment.

December 25, 1996: The Holy Family appeared dressed in robes of clearest and purest gold. Jesus and our Lady showed their Sacred Hearts and pointed, with their hands, to the Heart of St. Joseph, which appeared surrounded by twelve white lilies and, within it, the Cross of Christ which surmounted the letter "M" (for Mary), formed as though by wounds. The twelve white lilies represent the purity and holiness of the Heart of St. Joseph: who has always been pure, chaste and holy to the greatest degree. The twelve lilies also represent the twelve tribes of Israel, one of which was the House of the patriarch Joseph. The Cross and the "M" of Mary inscribed in the Heart of St. Joseph, represents his devoted and wholehearted love for Jesus and Mary. They are formed by wounds because St. Joseph shared in the sufferings of Jesus and Mary, also participating in the ministry of redemption.

From the Hearts of Jesus and Mary, rays of light shine towards the Heart of St. Joseph. These rays represent the love of the Triune Holy Hearts of Jesus, Mary and Joseph, just as the Holy Trinity is one and triune in love. The rays from the Hearts of Jesus and Mary direct us towards the Heart of St. Joseph in order to show us that he received all the graces and virtues of their most holy Hearts. For Jesus and Mary shared all with him and did not deny him anything, in gratitude for the devotedness of St. Joseph to them.

The rays coming out of the Heart of St. Joseph are all the graces, virtues, and holy love, which he received from the Hearts of Jesus and Mary, which he now pours forth over all those who invoke the aid of his Most Chaste Heart. This triune devotion of the Sacred Hearts of Jesus, Mary and Joseph, united in one love, glorify the Holy Trinity: one and triune.

March 1, 1998 – St. Joseph: In this apparition, St. Joseph appeared dressed in a white tunic with a blue robe, accompanied by several angels. St. Joseph held a lily bud and revealed to me his Heart.

"My dear son, our Lord God has sent me to tell you about all the graces the faithful will receive from my Most Chaste Heart which Jesus and my blessed spouse wish to be honoured. I am St. Joseph and my name means "God will grow," because I grew every day in grace and divine virtues. Through devotion to my Chaste Heart many souls will be saved from the hands of the Devil. God our Lord has allowed for me to reveal to you the promises of my Heart. Just as I am fair and righteous in the sight of God, all who have devotion to my Heart will also be chaste, righteous and holy in His sight. I will fill you with these graces and virtues, making you grow every day on the road of holiness. This is all I will reveal to you on this day. I give my blessing to you my son, and all mankind: in the name of the Father and of the Son and of the Holy Spirit. Amen."

March 2, 1998 – St. Joseph and the Child Jesus: St. Joseph appeared with the Child Jesus, with a red mantle and a white tunic. The Boy Jesus had His head inclined on St. Joseph's Heart, playing with the lilies he held in his hands. St. Joseph had brilliant green eyes and a beautiful smile – he appeared to be very young with an indescribable beauty.

The Child Jesus: "My son, behold this heart ..." With one of His little hands, the Child Jesus opened the illuminated chest of St. Joseph. In His other hand, Jesus held the Most Chaste Heart of St. Joseph.

"Here in this Heart you will find me living, because it is pure and saintly. That all hearts could be like this one, so they could be My home on earth. Imitate this Heart so that you may receive My graces and blessings."

St. Joseph: "My beloved son, today I bless you, I bless your mother and all your family. My beloved Son, God our Lord, wishes to give all humanity countless graces, through devotion to my heart. My son and Lord Jesus, that I brought up here on earth with a father's love, desires that all men practice devotion to my Heart, for all those in need of graces from Heaven. He also asks that men help others in need with their good deeds. I promise to all that honour this Most Chaste Heart of mine, and who do here on earth good deeds in favour of the most needy, especially of the sick and dying for whom I am a consoler and protector, to receive in their last moment of their lives the grace of a good death. I myself will be to these souls their petitioner to my Son Jesus and, together with my spouse, Most Holy Mary, we will console them in their last hours here on earth with our holy presence, and they will rest in the peace of our Hearts.

Just as you saw my Son Jesus repose His head on my Heart, this way myself and my spouse Holy Mary will take these souls to the glory of paradise, in the presence of their Saviour, my Son Jesus Christ, so that they may repose, and incline themselves to His Sacred Heart, in the burning furnace of the most pure and loving Heart. I give you my blessing: in the name of the Father and the Son and the Holy Spirit. Amen."

March 3, 1998 – St. Joseph: St. Joseph came dressed in a white tunic and a white cloak, holding a lily and the Child Jesus, also in white, on his lap.

"My beloved son, listen and make it known to all men what God has permitted me to reveal to you. My beloved son, how sin spreads in a such a strong way! Men allow themselves to be led by the most insidious wiles of the devil. The enemy of salvation wants to destroy all men so that, this way, all will be lost. He is envious and hates the entire human race. So many go through trials and temptations, that the enemy of God throws at every moment, this way trying to destroy men's mortal souls that were created by God.

The means that he most utilizes are the sins against holy purity, because purity is one of the virtues most beloved by God, and in this way, Satan desires to destroy the image of God present in each creature through this virtue. And it is because of this that God asks all humanity to have devotion to my Chaste Heart, He wants to give men the grace to overcome the temptations and attacks of the Devil in their day to day lives.

The invocation of my name is enough to make demons flee! I promise to all the faithful that honour my Most Chaste Heart with faith and love, the grace to live with holy purity of soul and body and the strength to resist all attacks and temptations by the Devil. I myself will preciously protect you. This grace is not only destined for those who honour this Heart of mine, but also for all their family members who need divine help. I give you my blessing: in the name of the Father and of the Son and of the Holy Spirit. Amen."

March 4, 1998 – St. Joseph: St. Joseph came dressed in a wine-coloured cloak with a green tunic. He held a staff in his right hand and showed his Chaste Heart streaming intense rays of light.

"My beloved son today is the first Wednesday of the month. On every first Wednesday of the month, my Chaste Heart pours numerous graces on all who rely on my intercession. On these Wednesdays, men will receive strong torrents of extraordinary graces! I will share them with those who honour me and rely on me: all the blessings, all the virtues, and all the love I received from my Divine Son Jesus and my spouse the Blessed Virgin Mary while still living in this world and all the graces that I continue to receive in the glory of paradise.

My beloved son, what a great honour and dignity I received from the Heavenly Father, that made my Heart exult with joy! The Heavenly Father granted me the honour of representing Him, in this world, to take care of His Divine and Beloved Son, Jesus Christ. My Heart was also surprised by so such dignity, I felt incapable and undeserving of such a great favour and benefit, but I put all in the hands of the Lord and, as His servant, I was ready to do His holy will. Think, my beloved son, what joy I felt in my Heart! The Son of the Most High was now in my care and was known by all men as my legitimate son. To the eyes of the world it was impossible, but for God everything is possible when He so desires it.

Because of this great grace and joy that God granted my Heart, I promise to intercede before Him for those who come to me, honouring this Heart of mine. I will give them the graces to be able to resolve the most difficult problems and urgent necessities, that to the eyes of man seem impossible, but that, through my intercession to God, will be possible. I grant the graces of my Heart to all sinners so they may convert. My Heart grants its rays of love on the entire Holy Church, particularly on my Son's Vicar, Pope John Paul II*. No one, such as he, has special access to this Heart of mine. That he may trust in my Heart and in my intercession, I am to the Holy Father as father and protector. I give my blessing: in the name of the Father and the Son and the Holy Spirit. Amen."

*8/15/89, Pope John Paul II released the Apostolic Exhortation REDEMPTORIS CUSTOS (Guardian of the Redeemer) that speaks of the life and mission of St. Joseph.

March 5, 1998 – The Holy Family: St. Joseph was in a beige cloak and blue grey tunic, in his arms was the Child Jesus wearing a very bright blue tunic. Our Lady was in a white veil and blue grey dress.

St. Joseph: "My beloved son, my Heart desires to spill many graces this night on all men, because I desire the conversion of all sinners so that they may be saved. That all sinners may not be afraid to approach my Heart, I desire to welcome and protect them. Many are those who are distant from God because of their grave sins. Many of those, my children, are in that state because they let themselves fall to the wiles of the devil. The enemy of salvation makes them think there is no solution, nor return, because they have despaired and have not trusted in Divine Mercy. These will be easy targets for the devil.

But I tell all sinners, even those who have committed the most terrible sins, to trust in the love and in the forgiveness of God and to trust in me also, in my intercession. All those who trustingly have recourse to me will have the certainty of my help to recover the divine grace and mercy of God. Look, my son, what the Heavenly Father entrusted to me to take care of: His Divine Son Jesus Christ and the Immaculate spouse of the Holy Spirit.

My Heart felt a great peace and joy for having Jesus and Mary at my side in the same house. Our three Hearts loved one another. We lived a trinitarian love, but it was a love united in the act of offering to the Eternal Father. Our Hearts melted into the purest love as though becoming one heart living in three persons.

But look, my son, how much my heart grieved and suffered in seeing my Son Jesus so little and already in danger for His life because of Herod that, taken by an evil spirit, ordered the killing of the innocent children. My heart went through great tribulation and suffering because of the great danger my Son Jesus suffered, but our Heavenly Father did not abandon us in that moment, He sent His messenger angel to direct me and to reveal to me what attitude to take in those difficult moments of suffering. Because of this, my son, tell all sinners to not despair in the great dangers of life and of the dangers of losing one's soul.

I promise all who will trust in my Most Chaste Heart, devoutly honouring it, the grace to be consoled by me in their greatest afflictions of the soul and in the danger of judgment, when by misfortune lose divine grace because of their grave sins. To these sinners, who have recourse to me, I promise the graces of my Heart for the purpose of amendment, of repentance and of sincere contrition of their sins. Now, I say to all sinners: Do not be afraid of the devil and do not despair because of your crimes, but come throw yourselves in my arms and take refuge in my Heart so that you may receive all the graces for your eternal salvation. Now I will give the world my blessing: in the name of the Father and of the Son and of the Holy Spirit. Amen."

March 6, 1998 – St. Joseph: "My beloved son, I would like to speak anew about the graces my Chaste Heart wishes to shower upon all humanity. My Chaste Heart, by the impulse of love, searches all ways to save all men from sin. My Son Jesus, through my Heart, wishes to impart to all men His divine blessings. I know many of you suffer many great difficulties because, in these last times, men no longer love or help one another but live with their hearts full of pride, falsehood, lies, intrigue, ambition, backbiting, pettiness, and many wrongs that are the consequences of living far from God.

My son, look at how much I suffered beside my Son Jesus and my Spouse the Blessed Virgin Mary! Like I have told you, I received from God the mission to be the guardian and protector of Jesus and Mary. My Heart was anguished because we did not live in the best of conditions in life, though I searched for a way to give a dignified life to the Son of the Most High.

The only means I had to bring home our daily bread was through my work as a carpenter. Work did not always have its adequate profit. Life had its problems, but I always trusted in Divine Providence. This was always our assistance for what was necessary for the survival of my beloved Son Jesus Christ. My Heart would become distressed because I felt I was not giving my Son Jesus a dignified life. God permitted me to go through this so that I would grow to trust in His Divine Providence. The virtue of humility would adorn my soul and I would be an example to all men and workers, so that they would also fulfill their duties and work with patience and love.

My beloved son, to all who honour this Heart of mine and trust in me and in my intercession, I promise they will not be abandoned in their difficulties and in the trials of life. I will ask our Lord to help them with His Divine Providence in their material and spiritual problems.

Mothers and fathers, consecrate yourselves to my Heart, likewise your families, and you will receive my help in your afflictions and problems. Just as I brought up the Son of the Most High in His holy laws, I will assist you with the upbringing and education of your children. I will help all fathers and mothers that consecrate their children to me, to bring them up with love in the holy laws of God, so they may find the secure road to salvation.

Now I tell all men: consecrate yourselves to my Chaste Heart. Consecrate all to me: your lives, your families, your jobs. Consecrate all to me, because my Heart is the new font of graces that God concedes to all humanity. I extend my cloak over the whole world and all the Holy Church. Trust in me and you will receive all graces. I give you my blessing: in the name of the Father and of the Son and of the Holy Spirit. Amen."

March 7, 1998 – St. Joseph: St. Joseph came in a leaf-green cloak and dark gray tunic. Our Blessed Mother came in a blue mantle and white dress with a white veil. The Child Jesus came in a light-yellow tunic. St. Joseph held the right hand of the Child Jesus.

"My beloved son, this night I, my Son Jesus and my spouse the Blessed Virgin, bless you in the name of the Father, of the Son and of the Holy Spirit. My beloved son, Jesus is very indignant with the sins of humanity.

He desires to pour His divine justice upon all men that do not want to repent and continue obstinately in their sins. Look, my son, I hold His right hand, preventing Him from pouring out His justice upon all humanity. I ask Him, through the graces of my Heart and for being worthy to live by His side, taking care of Him with the love of a father in this world, and for Him having loved me with the love of a son, to not chastise the world for its crimes, but for all my little ones who honour this Chaste Heart of mine, should pour out His mercy upon the world.

How many sins are committed in the world, my son! It is necessary that men do much penance, that they repent of their errant attitudes, because God receives continued offenses from ungrateful men. Today there are so many outrages, the sacrilege and indifference by all men. It is because of this that so many calamities like war, hunger and disease occur and so many other sad things man has suffered because of man's rebellion against God.

God lets men follow their own paths to show them all, without Him, they will never be happy. He lets men go through so much suffering to also show them the consequences sin brings to their lives and so then the Divine Justice punishes humanity because of their obstinance in not being obedient to God's Will. Because of this, my beloved son, in these last times, humanity grows increasingly obstinate in their crimes, because what matters most for him are the pleasures of worldly things, rather than the love of God and His Commandments. But God's justice is close at hand in a way never seen before and will come about suddenly upon the whole world.

So then, my son, tell all those that honour this Chaste Heart of mine they will receive the grace of my protection from all evils and dangers. For those who surrender to me will not be slaughtered by misfortunes, by wars, hunger, by diseases and other calamities, they will have my Heart as a refuge for their protection. Here, in my Heart, all will be protected against the Divine Justice in the days that will come. All who consecrate themselves to my Heart, honouring it, they will be looked upon by my Son Jesus with eyes of mercy. Jesus will pour out His love and will take to the glory of His Kingdom all those I put in my Heart. This is my message for tonight. I bless you: In the name of the Father and of the Son and of the Holy Spirit. Amen."

March 8, 1998 – St. Joseph: St. Joseph was dressed in a dark maroon tunic and light maroon cloak, surrounded by twelve angels with large wings.

"My beloved son, my Heart exults in joy by these encounters, I want to pour out these graces that the Lord has permitted me to give. I want, through my Heart, to lead all men to God. Here, in my Heart, all men are protected and through it they will understand the love of God in their lives.

My son, all those who propagate the devotion to my Heart, and practice it with love, have the certainty of having their names engraved on it just as my Son Jesus' cross and the "M" of Mary are engraved on it, as formed by wounds. This also applies for all priests whom I love with predilection. The priests who have a devotion to my Heart and spread it will have the grace of touching the most hardened hearts and convert obstinate sinners. That all may spread devotion to my Heart, it is God Himself who asks it. For all those who listen to my plea, I give my blessing.

You are to spread this devotion to all men, my beloved son, as you are designated by God to be the apostle of my Heart. Tell everyone of my love! Later I will come to speak to you about other things that will be very important for the salvation of many souls. God has entrusted you with a great mission – trust in me and you will know how to truly realize it. I give you my blessing: in the name of the Father of the Son and of the Holy Spirit. Amen.

March 9, 1998 – Our Lady: St. Joseph came, in a burgundy cloak and white tunic, with Our Lady, in a blue mantle and white dress. The Child Jesus, all in white, was sitting on St. Joseph's lap.

"My beloved son, this night I, my Son Jesus and my Most Chaste Spouse St. Joseph, bless the whole world. I ask you to listen and to live the holy messages of God. Continue to pray the holy Rosary every day and, particularly, beloved son, the seven Apostles' Creeds, because here in the Amazon there will be a great loss of faith. It is because of this I ask you to always pray the seven Creeds, since many will lose their faith and abandon the Holy Church in the difficult moments to come. I, your Mother, ask you to continue to pray to prevent that great danger and those difficult days during which many will suffer.

All who honour the Most Chaste Heart of St. Joseph will benefit with my maternal presence in their lives in a special way. I will be at the side of each son and daughter of mine, helping and comforting them with a mothers' heart, just as I helped and comforted my Most Chase Spouse Joseph in this world. To those who ask of his Heart with trust, I promise to intercede before the Eternal Father, my Divine Son Jesus and the Holy Spirit. I will obtain for them, from God, the grace to reach perfect sanctity in the virtues of St. Joseph, this way reaching the perfect love in which he lived. Men will learn to love my Son Jesus and myself with the same love as my Most Chaste Spouse Joseph, receiving the most pure love from our Hearts.

My Son Jesus, my Chaste Spouse Joseph and I are at your side. Fear nothing, because our Hearts will protect you always. I give you my blessing: in the name of the Father and of the Son and of the Holy Spirit. Amen."

March 10, 1998 – Our Lord Jesus: Jesus was majestically dressed. He spoke with great love and royal authority. He was beautiful and full of light that radiated from His being, as if the light was coming out from within and permanently surrounding Him. Each time He spoke about the devotion to His Virginal Father Joseph's Heart, His countenance became illuminated and His Heart shone the greater.

"My beloved son, today I pour out all the graces of my Heart and I bless all humanity. I desire that all men have devotion to the Most Chaste Heart of my Virginal Father Joseph. Those that will honour him, as they do My Heart, will bring Me joy. Speak to all men about this devotion that has been revealed to you. You should love my Virginal Father Joseph as I love him, because, in loving him, you will be doing My will and imitating Me in all.

I want to save all sinners, I love everyone. I am your God, I created you and I want you to be happy by My side and to share in My love and in the glory of paradise. Because of this, all who will honour My Virginal Father Joseph's Heart, will receive at the hour of death the grace to resist the schemes of the enemy of salvation, receiving victory and the deserved recompense in the Kingdom of My Heavenly Father. Those who devoutly honour this Chaste Heart in this world have the certainty of receiving great glory in Heaven.

The devoted souls of My Virginal Father Joseph will benefit from the beatific vision of the Holy Trinity and will have the profound knowledge of the One Triune God, the thrice Holy. They will enjoy the presence of My Heavenly Mother and My Virginal Father Joseph in the heavenly Kingdom. These souls will be loved by the Holy Trinity and by My Holy Mother Mary and will incircle the Most Chaste Heart of my Virginal Father Joseph like the most beautiful of lilies. I bless you, my beloved son, your whole family, and the whole world: in the name of the Father and of the Son and of the Holy Spirit. Amen."

March 19, 1998 – Our Lady and St. Joseph: The Holy Family appeared to me this day: Our Lady with St. Joseph, who was holding the Child Jesus in his arms. All three were dressed in gold. The Child Jesus had His back to me, with His little arms around St. Joseph's neck, with His head down as if crying, asking for comfort and support.

Our Lady: "My Son is very saddened by all the young people, because the young people of today offend Him with grave sins and do not want to know of God, rebelling against Him. Jesus is saddened by all those persons who do not want to change their lives by repenting of their sins."

St. Joseph: "My heart greatly yearns for the salvation of all. Take from my Heart all the graces that you need for your salvation. I give my blessing to you and to the world."

July 15, 2000: After Mass, when I was praying the Rosary, God revealed to me something about the union of the three Hearts of Jesus, Mary and Joseph. First, I was given to understand the union of St. Joseph in the mystery of the Incarnation. With each joyful mystery of the Rosary I began understanding the participation of St. Joseph in the work of redemption: in the Annunciation, the Visitation, in the Nativity, the Presentation and in the Loosing and Finding of Jesus in the Temple.

I saw the radiant Chaste Heart of St. Joseph wrapped in light. This vision caused in me great contemplation and made me understand how much St. Joseph's Heart is full of love and grace, and how much God desires to concede many graces and light to mankind for their salvation. In seeing this vision, I felt totally wrapped and absorbed by the presence of God who performed great wonders in St. Joseph, and I knew something about his great sanctity, glory and power that men ignore. How God desires that men make use of this great font of graces, but they reject it.

After this, I saw the three Hearts of Jesus, Mary and Joseph that were united as one. This vision repeated three times so that the significance would be well understood. It was one radiant and luminous Heart that lived with intense love and unity, honouring, adoring and glorifying the Holy Trinity in everything.

Immediately following this, I saw a large eye: it was the Eye of God that sees all. I felt a great and holy fear. I felt very small. Through that eye I saw my nothingness and my weakness, and I asked God pardon of my defects. I was enlightened concerning the majesty of God who is Omnipotent, Omnipresent and Omniscient and all this was impressed on my mind and in my soul.

Then appeared to me St. Joseph, with a beautiful paternal smile who showed me his Most Chaste Heart. I understood that his bond and union with the Father is very great and intimate, because it was the Father who chose him to represent Him on this earth in his paternity for His Divine Son Jesus. St. Joseph blessed me and disappeared.

After this I saw the Hand of God, in the form of the Trinity, who also blessed me. I understood that the Father blessed jointly with St. Joseph, so that I would be fortified to carry out the mission that he confided to me: to spread the devotion of this Chaste Heart.

January 21, 2003: At night I saw St. Joseph, who came to bless us: He showed me his Chaste Heart which gave off many rays of light. He showed me a vision: St. Joseph entered the doors of St. Peter's Basilica at the Vatican and from inside he blessed the Church and the world. After this, I saw St. Joseph showing the Pope his Chaste Heart, embracing him afterwards.

June 20, 2007 – St. Joseph: "Peace be with you! My children, I am the blessed spouse of the Blessed Virgin and the righteous one of the Lord. I come this night with my Divine Son to grant the graces that God has permitted me to distribute to all those who honour and celebrate my Most Chaste Heart. My Heart exults in joy this night, to see you united here in prayer. I tell you my little ones, those who seek my help and intercession will not be abandoned by me. I desire to take all men to Jesus and Mary. These are times of great graces. I love you and I tell you to make of your lives a gift of love to God, just as I offered my life to Him from my infancy.

Pray for those who live in the darkness of sin. So many souls are destroyed by sin. The devil is enraged and desires to show his shameful face in Brazil with violence and hatred. Pray to stop him by your fasting and prayers, because, if you do not listen to my pleading, you will see many sorrowful things happen in your country.

... So many priests are in darkness, because they do not pray and are not faithful to God. Today many of the priest's homilies do not touch the hearts of the faithful, in converting them, because many of their souls are rotten with sin. Whoever is in sin cannot receive the grace and light of God to illuminate others. Jesus said: can the blind lead the blind? No, beloved children. If you want to be a light to your brothers, you must convert yourselves first and repent of your sins and in this way the grace of God will envelope you.

My Heart loves God and the Blessed Virgin so very much. If you want to belong to them, approach my Heart and I will teach you to love them. I give you my blessing – a blessing of peace and of love, united to my Son: in the name of the Father and of the Son and of the Holy Spirit. Amen."

June 24, 2009 – St. Joseph: Today St. Joseph appeared, with the Child Jesus and our Lady, all dressed in gold. They showed me their Hearts. They were surrounded by many angels and saints. St. Joseph was the one who gave me the message this night:

"The peace of Jesus to you all! My son, today my Most Chaste Heart is joyful with the presence of all who came to honour me with their prayers. My Son Jesus permits me to grant you numerous graces this blessed night on which he desired to dedicate to my Chaste Heart (the first Wednesday after the Feast of the Sacred Heart of Jesus). Praise and bless the Holy Name of the Lord who does great things and wonders.

The families who deliver themselves to my protection will not be turned away from God, because I will lead them to Him. I come from Heaven with my Heart full of love. My Divine Son blesses you and my Immaculate Spouse will shelter you under her pure and holy mantle. Love Jesus and Mary and teach this to your brothers. Today, Heaven is in celebration with all the angels and saints praising my Most Chaste Heart which God has granted to me. All the angels and saints are praying with you all and accompany you. Have faith. Many graces are being dispensed to all of you. Welcome the messages from Heaven and you will find Salvation. I give my blessing to all: in the name of the Father and of the Son and of the Holy Spirit. Amen."

December 13, 2009 – St. Joseph: Today St. Joseph, who had his Most Chaste Heart exposed, came with the Child Jesus, surrounded with very beautiful angels. St. Joseph was in a white cloak and white tunic and the Child Jesus in a light blue tunic with little shinning stars.

"The peace of Jesus be with you all! My beloved son, today the Lord has sent me from Heaven to bless you all. You and your brothers must understand the great graces He sends you. They are special graces. My presence here this night is a great gift from God for all of humanity. As I have told you, He wants to make me well known and loved in the world. I am here before you with my Most Chaste Heart full of the Omnipotent's love. Pray always and trust. Trust and faith attract great blessings from Heaven. God is calling you to Himself – return now! He is merciful and compassionate. His Divine Heart is full of love for you.

My son, God made great wonders in my life. Of all men he honoured me, glorified me and benefited me with His grace. In truth, what a great grace He gave me in having Jesus and Mary by my side, whom I loved so much in this world. How many blessings, graces and virtues my Heart received from their Most Holy Hearts! My life on earth was a continued ecstasy of love. My soul would enter in the most profound contemplation of the mysteries of God, of His salvific works. My soul and my heart were profoundly united to Jesus and Mary.

All my being belonged to them for I dedicated my life to them – realizing the will of the Father, guided by the Holy Spirit. My son, the days spent at the side of Jesus and Mary in Nazareth were the most sublime and holy. My soul was included in this mystery of love, being sanctified more and more as our Lord desired it. And when the time came, the hour of my death was a true ecstasy of love.

After my death I stayed in a place reserved by the Lord, being the one that illuminated all the blessed and elect of God until the moment of the resurrection of my Divine Son Jesus.

On the day of the resurrection of Jesus, the Lord crowned my soul and my body in glory. He took me to Heaven on the day of His ascension and holy is His Name. Hosanna to the One who is, who was, and who will come!

My son, speak to all of my glories and virtues. It is God's will that you manifest it to the world. Pray, pray, pray and God will illuminate you. I am at your side and I bless you, as well as all humanity: in the name of the Father, of the Son and of the Holy Spirit. Amen."

MANAUS, BRAZIL 1991 – Present
Witness: Larissa Baptista

Since 1991 Larissa Baptista is said to have been receiving messages from Jesus, Mary, and Joseph. The phenomenon occurs in the form of an inner locution when she prays. Larissa is also said to receive interior visions which she says are imprinted on her soul and intellect.

Inner locution is common in the Church. Saints Catherine of Sienna, Teresa of Avila, John of the Cross, and many others, are examples of how God manifests Himself and continues to act through internal visions and locutions. On August 27, 2018, these visions and messages were given Church approval by Archbishop Sergio Eduardo Castriani. What follows are messages pertaining to St. Joseph:

St. Joseph – Manaus, 08/03/2016: "Peace be with you and with your family. I, Joseph, come from God to exhort you to trust in my Son, as I trust. I come to help lift your spirits in the face of despair. In these times when children are particularly mistreated, persecuted, I come as an effective aid to fight against Herod who continues to dissipate the children. Your sons and your daughters are in danger, your children are leaving the family very early to throw themselves into the world that kills them. Yes, the children are dying in their innocence, in their purity.

I come then to introduce myself to them as an effective help in these times of great danger. I also wish to be known as the father and protector of children. As I defended my Son, so too do I desire to defend and protect your children. I am the defender of the defenseless little children; I am the great and present warrior that fights the evil Herod. Make me known as the protector of children, I will keep them in my Heart which is united to the Hearts of Jesus and Mary – pulsating together with the desire to make your children holy."

St. Joseph – Manaus, 09/03/2016: "Peace be with you and with your family. I come again to tell you God's desire that I become known and loved among children. I wish to be their protection in moments of danger. I desire that everyone, even children, recognize my Chaste and Virginal Heart as your haven.

Boys who are consecrated to me …

1. Will receive from God the grace to be His joy on earth as I was.

2. Will receive special graces to follow their vocations with fidelity to God without ever departing from the Divine Laws.

3. Boys who have a devotion to my Chaste Heart will not offend God with the sin of impurity and will reject all kinds of filth that the world tries to cover their souls with.

4. These boys will have the grace, if it is the will of God, to become exemplary parents and husbands faithful to the Divine Laws.

5. They will have the grace, as I do, to be fathers, protectors, and caretakers of their families.

Consecrate your children to my Chaste and Virginal Heart."

Larissa: And the girls, Saint Joseph? What do you have for them?

1. "The purity of soul and body. They will be as wives of the Lord and will follow their vocations, belonging to God in their innocence.

2. The girls who consecrate themselves to me will have my paternal protection until the end of their days.

3. They will be comforted by me in their afflictions and will never see the days of darkness without my protection.

4. Daughters who consecrate themselves to me will have strength, courage to face all kinds of situations without ever losing their patience, courage and faith. I myself will carry you as I did my Divine Son.

5. I will comfort you and watch over your physical and spiritual integrity. I will be your protector on Earth and in Heaven.

Propagate, my daughter, this salutary devotion of the children to my Chaste and Virginal Heart. I bless you with the blessing of peace."

Our Lord Jesus – Manaus, 10/03/2016: "My daughter, I promise to whoever devotes themselves to Joseph, a particular wisdom not granted to those who do not place their confidence in him. Behold, though I am God, I submitted to his teachings to show that this is a sure way to reach Heaven. Joseph's Heart is an inexhaustible source of grace because it is nourished by My Sacred Heart and by the Heart of the one who accompanied Me in submitting to Joseph: Mary. Have complete confidence in him who loved Me on Earth and who does not leave My presence in Heaven. Saint Joseph is a strong presence in these times of danger. Many graces will be attained for those who seek them from his Paternal Heart."

Larissa: Lord, is St. Joseph as holy as Your Mother?

Jesus: "Indeed. Just as my Mother reflects my light, so too does he reflect hers' and mine."

St. Joseph – Manaus, 19/03/2016: While praying the Joyful Mysteries of the Rosary, I saw the boy Joseph who held a lit candle in his right hand and a cross in the left. St. Joseph said:

"My heart was full of innocence, not a childish innocence, but an innocence that surpassed the wisest of the earth."

At the fourth mystery, I saw Jesus, Mary, and Joseph – all three as children. I realized that Joseph was taller than Mary and Jesus. Jesus was much lower than both. At this moment I remembered the great humility of Jesus, that by being Great, He became the smallest out of humility.

At the fifth mystery, as I meditated on the loss and finding of the Child Jesus, I felt a pain in my chest, a sadness, then I heard St. Joseph again, saying:

"During the moments when my Son was lost, my Heart bled. I realized my smallness in taking care of the Son of God. I could not do it without His grace."

God allowed me to see St. Joseph's great humility before the mystery to which he was invited to participate. I then knelt and I saw our Lady, as an adult, who gently placed her hands on the back of St. Joseph and pushed him gently forward, as if introducing me. He wore a light green tunic with a golden collar. His face was thin, his hair was light brown and wavy. He carried a large lily in his hands. St. Joseph spoke:

"Peace be with you, daughter of the Most-High, peace to all mankind! On this day, honoured as Patron of the Church, I come to tell you that I am truly the Protector and Guardian not only of the Church of Christ, but also of the church that is your home.

Holy as I am, by the power and goodness of the Most-High, I wish to sanctify your homes, leaving with each family a piece of the Heaven that I lived in Nazareth. I am the patron of your family, I want to help you live the in the ways of the Most-High, as I have lived. Be therefore docile, in these times when the Church of Christ is vilified, be docile to His Word.

I want to reveal to you the sweetness and simplicity of my boyish Heart. I received from God at an early age the grace of wisdom that surpasses the wisest of the Earth, a gift that God has communicated to me which I communicate to the Church. Today my Heart holds you, Larissa, and I want you to reveal my Heart to the world without fear. I have, and always did have, an innocent Heart: innocent in love and pure of spirit. There is no innocence without true love for God. I had an innocent Heart from an early age. Cultivate this innocence as a child and you will see God. Communicate to the people that I establish with them my eternal friendship."

St. Joseph – Manaus, 31/08/2016: "I give to you an effective formula for consecrating your children to me:

O Glorious Saint Joseph, loving Father of the Child God. I give to you this day my life and everything that belongs to it. Take care of my body (+) so that I never lose childlike purity, take care of my ears (+) my eyes (+) and my mouth (+) so that they will perpetually maintain innocence in their natural acts. Keep me from the adversaries of my soul so that I may keep and persevere in the faith. Above all, St. Joseph, guard my heart in yours and I will keep my innocence, that I may reach Heaven. Saint Joseph father of Jesus, and my friend, guard me.

This consecration should be done after three days of meditation on the footsteps of my life. Write down:

1. Joy I had in knowing that Mary begot the Son of God and consequently that I would have Him in my arms.

2. Joy I felt when I saw Him wrapped in swaddling clothes and placed in my paternal arms.

3. Joy I experienced with Him after three days of cruel pursuit by Herod's soldiers.

Let them meditate on my steps and pray. At the end of three consecutive days may they be consecrated to my Heart."

St. Joseph – Manaus, 09/09/2016: "Come, my daughter, and write what God wants to speak, through me, as a gift to humanity. Three are the most perfect virtues that have adorned my Heart, three perfumed lilies that put the demon to flight. I want you to honour my Heart as a balm for suffering humanity.

My Heart has three stars upon it: The first star honours my holy birth. The second honours my life with my beloved spouse: the Holy Virgin who perfumed my days on earth and now in paradise. The third star honours my death and definitive encounter with my Saviour. All these perfected my life on earth and guaranteed my life in Heaven.

My Heart holds, in its center, the cross of my Son Jesus who is the center of, and only reason for, my life. He was born in God and for God. The birth of the God-Child brought to my Heart the divine flames which issue forth from it. The Holy Spirit came into my Heart to prepare me to receive the One who would save mankind. I am the child who was sanctified by the Spirit in love."

St. Joseph – Manaus, 10/09/2016: "Peace be with you, little one, do not be frightened, I let you sleep a little longer. I thank you for what you are doing for Heaven. God will reward you greatly. You were chosen, by God, to bring to humanity to the knowledge of my Chaste and Virginal Heart and all that it wishes to reveal.

Be glad! Today, I will reveal to you the graces that are poured out on humanity every time my Childlike Heart is honoured:

1. I will never cease to hear your prayers and, if it is the will of God, to grant those petitions through my Chaste Heart.

2. You will be strong when faced with tribulation and I will defend, with the purity of my innocence, all those who call to me through my Chaste and Childlike Heart.

3. My Childlike Heart is a sure source for salvation, for I carry Christ in my Heart.

Two virtues are intrinsic in my Chaste and Virginal Heart: chastity and virginity, I never wanted to lose these qualities, not that those who no longer possess these are not good, but it was God's will for me to retain these.

St. Joseph – Manaus, 10/09/2016: Prayer taught by St. Joseph:

O Joseph, chaste and virginal man. Your Childlike Heart is a refuge for my Soul. Your Holy Childhood inspires my life that, in this vale of tears, I may always strive for salvation. Joseph, teach me your faith so that I will always escape anything that is contrary to my salvation.

Joseph, teach me the virtue of purity and chastity to please God in soul and body. Joseph, Childlike Heart, restore in my life the innocence of a child that pleases Heaven so much. You are my fragrant lily; you are my inspiration. You are the delicacy of all the Saints.

You are my strength in moments of danger. Joseph, with the Heart of a Child, defend my soul from the assaults of the devil. You are the beloved child of God. Saint Joseph, model of all virtues, help me to go to Heaven. Amen.

PART FIVE: RELICS

THE CLOAK OF ST. JOSEPH

St. Jerome, one of the great translators of the Bible, lived in Bethlehem where, for over 20 years, he lived with the early Christian community (4th century). While there, he had access to an incredible relic: The Cloak of St. Joseph. This important relic was safely kept until its move to the Basilica of Sant'Anastasia in Rome, where it has been housed with the mantle of the Virgin Mary for over 1600 years.

CINTURE OF ST. JOSEPH

In 1254, one of the great chroniclers of medieval France, Jean de Joinville, brought in from Jerusalem the belt of St. Joseph, for which a chapel was built in the Church of Notre-Dame de Joinville-sur-Marne. The Holy Cinture is roughly one and a half meters long, greyish in colour. The ends attach with an ivory clasp – yellowed by time. After the death of St. Joseph, it remained with the Virgin Mary. In the 13th century the belt was embroidered with Fleur de Lis emblems and verses from the Litany of St Joseph.

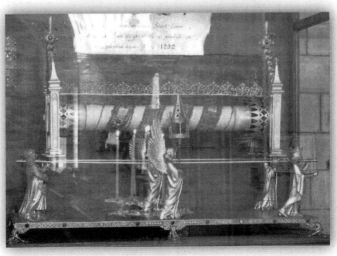

ROD OF ST. JOSEPH

The rod which sprouted blossoms at his espousal to Mary was used as a walking stick on the Holy family's journeys. Later, it was kept by Joseph of Arimathea after the death of St. Joseph. The relic was taken to England after the First Crusades and held at a monastery of the Carmelite Fathers in Sussex. In 1775 St. Joseph's rod was moved to Naples where it is still held in the Church of San Giuseppe dei Nudi.

VIRGIN MARY'S WEDDING RING GIVEN BY ST. JOSEPH

This quartz ring is said to have served as the wedding ring given by St. Joseph to the Blessed Virgin Mary. According to an 11th century account, a Jewish dealer in precious stones in Rome gave it to a jeweler from Chiusi, called Ainerio, in the late 10th century. He doubted its authenticity until his newly deceased young son was temporarily restored to life in order to vouch for it. It is currently housed in the Cappella del Santo Anello in Perugia, Italy.

STATUE CARVED BY ST. JOSEPH

According to tradition the statue of the Virgin Mary nursing the infant Jesus, known as Nossa Senhora de Nazaré (Our Lady of Nazareth), was carved by St. Joseph. The image was taken from the Holy Land in the 6th century to Spain, where it remained in a monastery near Merida until the year 711. It was then moved to Portugal after the Battle of Guadalete and remained hidden in a coastal cave until 1182 when it was found by the knight Dom Roupinho. The humble statue carved by St. Joseph, as a loving tribute to his wife and son, now resides in the baroque Santuário de Nossa Senhora da Nazaré.

PART SIX: POPES, SAINTS, & FEAST DAYS

Pope Francis, *Inaugural Mass 19 March 2013:* How does Joseph respond to his calling to be the protector of Mary, Jesus and the Church? By being constantly attentive to God, open to the signs of God's presence and receptive to God's plans, and not simply to his own. ... Joseph is a "protector" because he can hear God's voice and be guided by His will; and for this reason, he is all the more sensitive to the persons entrusted to his safekeeping. He can look at things realistically, he is in touch with his surroundings, and he can make truly wise decisions. In him, dear friends, we learn how to respond to God's call, readily and willingly, but we also see the core of the Christian vocation, which is Christ! Let us protect Christ in our lives, so that we can protect others, so that we can protect creation!

Pope Benedict XVI, *Homily 19 March 2009:* Each and every one of us has a role to play in the plan of God: Father, Son and Holy Spirit. If discouragement overwhelms you, think of the faith of Joseph; if anxiety has its grip on you, think of the hope of Joseph; if exasperation or hatred seizes you, think of the love of Joseph, who was the first man to set eyes on the human face of God in the person of the Infant conceived by the Holy Spirit in the womb of the Virgin Mary. Let us praise and thank Christ for having drawn so close to us, and for giving us Joseph as an example and model of love for Him.

St. Pope John Paul II, *Redemptoris*
Custos 15 August 1989: The
patronage of St. Joseph must be
invoked, and it is always necessary
for the Church, not only to defend it
against dangers ceaselessly cropping
up, but also and above all to support
it in those fearful efforts at evangelizing the world, and spreading
the new evangelization among nations where the Christian
religion and life were formerly the most flourishing, but are now
put to a difficult test... May St. Joseph become for all a singular
master in the service of the saving mission of Christ that is
incumbent on each and every one of us in the Church: to spouses,
to parents, to those who live by the work of their hands or by any
other work, to persons called to the contemplative life as well as
to those called to the apostolate.

St. Pope Paul VI, *Homily 19 March*
1969: The Church invokes St. Joseph
as her Patron and Protector through
Her unshakable trust that he to whom
Christ willed to confide the care and
protection of His own frail human
childhood, will continue from Heaven
to perform his protective task in order to guide and defend the
Mystical Body of Christ Himself, which is always weak, always
under attack, always in a state of peril. We call upon St. Joseph
for the world, trusting that the heart of the humble working man
of Nazareth, now overflowing with immeasurable wisdom and
power, still harbors and will always harbor a singular and
precious fellow-feeling for the whole of mankind. So, may it be.

St. Pope John XXIII, *Allocution 19 March 1959:* All the saints in glory assuredly merit honour and particular respect, but it is evident that, next to the Blessed Mother, Saint Joseph possesses a just title to a more sweet, more intimate and penetrating place in our hearts, belonging to him alone... We can see all the greatness of Saint Joseph, not only by reason of the fact that he was close to Jesus and Mary, but also by the shining example he has given of all virtues.

Venerable Pope Pius XII, *Address 1 May 1955:* St. Joseph is the best protector to help you in your life, to penetrate the spirit of the Gospel. Indeed, from the Heart of the God-Man, Saviour of the world, this spirit is infused in you and in all men, but it is certain that there was no worker's spirit so perfectly and deeply penetrated as the putative father of Jesus, who lived with Him in the closest intimacy and community of family and work. So, if you want to be close to Christ, I repeat to you "Ite ad Ioseph": Go to Joseph!

Pope Pius XI, *Divini Redemptoris 19 March 1937:* To hasten the advent of that "peace of Christ in the kingdom of Christ" so ardently desired by all, We entrust the vast campaign of the Church against world Communism under the standard of St. Joseph, Her mighty Protector. He belongs to the working-class, and he bore the burdens of poverty for himself and the Holy Family, whose tender and vigilant head he was. To him was entrusted the Divine Child when Herod loosed his assassins against Him. In a life of faithful performance of everyday duties, he left an example for all those who must gain their bread by the toil of their hands. He won for himself the title of "The Just," serving thus as a living model of that Christian justice which should reign in social life.

Pope Benedict XV, *Bonum Sane 25 July 1920:* We, full of confidence in the patronage of the one to whose provident supervision God was pleased to entrust the custody of His only-begotten Incarnate Son, and the Virgin Mother of God, we earnestly exhort all the Bishops of the Catholic world that, in times so turbulent for Christianity, to induce the faithful to  pray with greater commitment for the valuable help of St. Joseph. And since there are several ways approved by the Apostolic See with whom you can venerate the Holy Patriarch, especially every Wednesday throughout the year and month consecrated to him, We want, for every Bishop to heed these requests — that all these devotions, as much as possible, are practised in every diocese.

St. Pope Pius X, *Prayer 26 November 1906:* O Joseph, virgin father of Jesus, pure spouse of the Virgin Mary, pray for us daily to the Son of God, that, armed with the weapons of His grace, we may fight as we ought in life, and be crowned by Him in death. All for Jesus, all through Mary, all after

thine example, O Patriarch, St. Joseph. Such shall be my watchword in life and in death.

Pope Leo XIII, *Quamquam Pluries 15 August 1889:* The Blessed  Patriarch Joseph looks upon the multitude of Christians who make up the Church as confided especially to his trust – this limitless family spread over the earth, over which, because he is the spouse of Mary and the father of Jesus Christ, he holds, as it were, a paternal authority. It is, then, natural and worthy that as the Blessed Joseph ministered to all the needs of the family at Nazareth and girt it about with his protection, he should now cover with the cloak of his heavenly patronage and defend the Church of Jesus Christ.

Blessed Pope Pius IX, *Inclytum Patriarcham 7 July 1871:* In  these latter times in which a monstrous and most abominable war has been declared against the Church of Christ ... we should more efficaciously implore the compassion of God through the merits and intercession of Saint Joseph ... Hence, by a special decree ... We solemnly declare the blessed patriarch Joseph Patron of the Universal Church! ... O God, who in your ineffable providence was pleased to choose blessed Joseph as the spouse of your most holy mother, grant, we beseech you, that we may be made worthy to have him for our intercessor in Heaven whom we venerate as our protector on earth.

Venerable Maria de Agreda: I have discovered that the Most-High accorded to St. Joseph, certain privileges in favour of those who choose him for their intercessor, and who invoke him with devotion ... I entreat all the faithful children of the Holy Church to have a great devotion for this great saint.

St. André Bessette: When you invoke Saint Joseph, you don't have to speak much. You know your Father in Heaven knows what you need; well, so does His friend Saint Joseph. Tell him, "If you were in my place, Saint Joseph, what would you do? Well, pray for this in my behalf."

St. Alphonsus Liguori: There is no doubt about it: just as Jesus Christ wanted to be subject to Joseph on earth, so He does everything the saint asks of Him in Heaven. When Egypt was laid waste by the great famine, Pharaoh told his people, *Ite ad Joseph!* – Go to Joseph! So if we are in trouble, let us listen to the word of the Lord and take Pharaoh's advice; let us go to Joseph if we wish to be consoled ... Above all, I most strongly urge you to ask him for three special graces: forgiveness of sins, love of Jesus Christ, and a happy death.

St. Teresa de Ávila: I took for my advocate and comforter the glorious Saint Joseph, and commended myself fervently to him; ... His aid has brought me more good than I ever desired to receive from him. ... I am quite amazed at the great favours our Lord has given me, and the many dangers, both of soul and body, from which He has delivered me through the intercession of this blessed saint!

St. Josemaria Escrivá: St. Joseph protects those who revere him and accompanies them on their journey through this life – just as he protected and accompanied Jesus when He was growing up. As you get to know him, you discover that the holy patriarch is also a master of the interior life – for he teaches us to know Jesus and share our life with Him, and to realize that we are part of God's family.

St. Pio of Pietrelcina: St. Joseph, with the love and generosity with which he guarded Jesus, so too will he guard your soul. All the care that St. Joseph has for Jesus, he has for you and will always help you with his patronage. He will not allow your heart to be estranged from Jesus. Go to Joseph with extreme confidence!

ST. JOSEPH FEAST DAYS

This is the day which the Lord has made; let us rejoice and be glad in it (Psalm 118:24 NASB).

Solemnity of Saint Joseph – March 19

First inserted into the General Roman Calendar for celebration in 1621 by Pope Gregory XV, although this date had already been informally dedicated to St. Joseph as early as the 10th century. This date also fittingly serves as "Father's' Day" in some Catholic countries such as Portugal, Spain, and Italy.

St. Joseph Patron of the Universal Church – 3rd Wednesday after Easter

Between 1870 and 1955, this feast day celebrated the title given to St. Joseph by Pope Pius IX. It honours St. Joseph as the Protector of the Mystical Body of Christ which is the Universal Church. This feast was later removed in 1955 by Pope Pius XII.

St. Joseph the Worker – May 1

In 1955 Pope Pius XII established the Feast Day of "St. Joseph the Worker" to be celebrated annually on May 1. This date was specifically chosen to counteract the predominantly Socialist and Communist holiday "International Workers' Day," also known as "May Day." Pius XII encouraged labourers to look to St. Joseph as their model and to ask for his intercession in their work.

Death of St. Joseph – Abib 26 (July 20 – Julian Calendar, August 2 – Gregorian Calendar)

The feast of the holy death of St. Joseph, recognized by the Coptic Church.

St. Joseph the Betrothed – First Sunday after Christmas

St. Joseph is commemorated on the Sunday after the Nativity by the Eastern Churches. If there is no Sunday between December 25 and January 1, his feast day, along with King David and St. James the Greater, is held on December 26.

Espousals of Mary and Joseph – January 23

Approved in 1546 by Pope Paul III to celebrate the holy espousals of the Blessed Virgin Mary and St. Joseph.

Feast of the Holy Family – First Sunday after Christmas

This feast was instituted by Pope Leo XIII. Should there be no Sunday between Christmas and New Year's Day, the feast is held on December 30.

Every Wednesday

It is Roman Catholic tradition to honour St. Joseph, in some way, every Wednesday. This practice was especially recommended by Pope Benedict XV.

PART SEVEN: PRAYER & SCRIPTURE

PRAYER OF ST. POPE PIUS X – O Joseph, virgin father of Jesus, pure spouse of the Virgin Mary, pray for us daily to the Son of God, that, armed with the weapons of His grace, we may fight as we ought in life, and be crowned by Him in death. Amen.

ANCIENT PRAYER TO ST. JOSEPH – O St. Joseph, whose protection is so great, so strong, so prompt before the Throne of God, I place in you all my interests and desires. O St. Joseph, do assist me by your powerful intercession and obtain for me from your Divine Son all spiritual blessings through Jesus Christ, our Lord; so that, having engaged here below your Heavenly power, I may offer my thanksgiving and homage to the most loving of fathers. O St. Joseph, I never weary contemplating you and Jesus asleep in your arms. I dare not approach while He reposes near your heart. Press Him in my name and kiss His fine Head for me and ask Him to return the Kiss when I draw my dying breath. St. Joseph, Patron of departing souls, pray for us. Amen.

CONSECRATION TO ST. JOSEPH – Hail, glory of the patriarchs, steward of God's holy Church, who didst preserve the

Bread of Life and the Wheat of the Elect. O Blessed Joseph, faithful guardian of my Redeemer, Jesus Christ, protector of thy chaste spouse, the Virgin Mother of God, I choose thee this day to be my special patron and advocate, I consecrate myself to thee and I firmly resolve to honour thee all the days of my life. Therefore, I humbly beseech thee to receive me as thy client, to instruct me in every doubt, to comfort me in every affliction, to obtain for me, and for all, the knowledge and love of the Heart of Jesus, and finally to defend and protect me at the hour of my death. Amen.

MEMORARE TO ST. JOSEPH – Remember, O most chaste spouse of the Virgin Mary, that never was it known that anyone who implored your help and sought your intercession were left unassisted. Full of confidence in your power I fly unto you and beg your protection. Despise not, O Guardian of the Redeemer, my humble supplication, but in your bounty, hear and answer me. Amen.

TO THEE O BLESSED JOSEPH – PRAYER OF POPE LEO XIII TO BE RECITED ESPECIALLY AT THE CONCLUSION OF THE ROSARY

To thee, O blessed Joseph, do we come in our tribulation, and, having implored the help of thy most holy Spouse, we confidently invoke thy patronage also.

Through that charity which bound thee to the Immaculate Virgin Mother of God and through the paternal love with which thou embraced the Child Jesus, we humbly beg thee to graciously regard the inheritance which Jesus Christ has purchased by His Blood, and with thy power and strength to aid us in our necessities.

O most watchful Guardian of the Holy Family, defend the chosen children of Jesus Christ; O most loving father, ward off from us every contagion of error and corrupting influence; O our most mighty protector, be propitious to us and from Heaven assist us in our struggles with the powers of darkness; and, as once thou rescued the Child Jesus from deadly peril, so now protect God's Holy Church from the snares of the enemy and from all adversity; shield, too, each one of us by thy constant protection, so that, supported by thy example and thy aid, we may be able to live piously, to die holy, and to obtain eternal happiness in heaven. + Amen.

NOVENA PRAYER TO ST. JOSEPH – Saint Joseph, I, your unworthy child, greet you. You are the faithful protector and intercessor of all who love and venerate you. You know that I have special confidence in you and that, after Jesus and Mary, I place all my hope of salvation in you, for you are especially powerful with God and will never abandon your faithful servants. Therefore, I humbly invoke you and commend myself, with all who are dear to me and all that belong to me, to your intercession. I beg of you, by your love for Jesus and Mary, not to abandon me during life and to assist me at the hour of my death.

Glorious Saint Joseph, spouse of the Immaculate Virgin, obtain for me a pure, humble, charitable mind, and perfect resignation to the divine Will. Be my guide, my father, and my model through life that I may merit to die as you did in the arms of Jesus and Mary.

Loving Saint Joseph, faithful follower of Jesus Christ, I raise my heart to you to implore your powerful intercession in obtaining from the Divine Heart of Jesus all the graces necessary for my spiritual and temporal welfare, particularly the grace of a happy death, and the special grace I now implore: (Mention your request). Guardian of the Word Incarnate, I feel confident that your prayers in my behalf will be graciously heard before the throne of God. Amen.

THE PRAISES OF ST. JOSEPH

Hail Joseph, image of God the Father.

Hail Joseph, father of God the Son.

Hail Joseph, temple of the Holy Ghost.

Hail Joseph, beloved of the Holy Trinity.

Hail Joseph, most faithful helper in the great plan of Redemption.

Hail Joseph, most worthy spouse of the Virgin Mother.

Hail Joseph, father of all the faithful.

Hail Joseph, guardian of holy virgins.

Hail Joseph, greatest lover of poverty.

Hail Joseph, example of meekness and patience.

Hail Joseph, mirror of humility and obedience.

Blessed art thou among all men.

And blessed are thine eyes, which have seen what thou hast seen.

And blessed are thine ears, which have heard what thou hast heard.

And blessed are thy hands, which have touched the Word Incarnate.

And blessed are thine arms, which have carried the One Who carries all things.

And blessed is thy breast, on which the Son of God most sweetly reposed.

And blessed is thy heart, kindled with most ardent love.

And blessed be the Eternal Father, Who chose thee.

And blessed be the Son, Who loved thee.

And blessed be the Holy Ghost, Who sanctified thee.

And blessed be Mary, thy spouse, who loved thee as a spouse and a brother.

And blessed be the Angel, who guarded thee.

And blessed be forever all who bless thee and who love thee.

LITANY OF SAINT JOSEPH
LITANIAE SANCTE IOSEPH

The earliest known Litany of St. Joseph, attributed to the Carmelite Fr. Jerónimo Gracián, was published in Rome in 1597. Through the ensuing years, various litanies in St. Joseph's honour began to circulate among the different religious orders and the laity. It was not until March 18, 1909, that the Church, through Pope St. Pius X, approved and indulgenced a Litany of St. Joseph for public and private use. This official approval was granted by the Holy Father's personal devotion to St. Joseph, and in response to the petitions of the faithful.

Kyrie, eleison.	Lord, have mercy.
R. Kyrie, eleison.	**R.** Lord, have mercy,
Christe, eleison.	Christ, have mercy.

R. Christe, eleison.	**R.** Christ, have mercy.
Kyrie, eleison.	Lord, have mercy.
R. Kyrie, eleison.	**R.** Lord, have mercy.
Christe, audi nos.	Christ, hear us.
R. Christe, exaudi nos.	**R.** Christ, graciously hear us.
Pater de caelis, Deus,	God the Father of Heaven,
R. miserere nobis.	**R.** have mercy on us.
Fili, Redemptor mundi, Deus,	God the Son, Redeemer of the world,
R. miserere nobis.	**R.** have mercy on us.
Spiritus Sancte Deus,	God the Holy Spirit,
R. miserere nobis.	**R.** have mercy on us.
Sancta Trinitas, unus Deus,	Holy Trinity, one God,
R. miserere nobis.	**R.** have mercy on us.
Sancta Maria,	Holy Mary,
R. ora pro nobis.	**R.** pray for us.
Sancte Ioseph,	St. Joseph,
R. ora pro nobis.	**R.** pray for us.
Proles David inclyta,	Renowned offspring of David,
R. ora pro nobis.	**R.** pray for us.

Lumen Patriarcharum,	Light of Patriarchs,
R. ora pro nobis.	**R.** pray for us.
Dei Genetricis Sponse,	Spouse of the Mother of God,
R. ora pro nobis.	**R.** pray for us.
Custos pudice Virginis,	Chaste guardian of the Virgin,
R. ora pro nobis.	**R.** pray for us.
Filii Dei nutricie,	Foster father of the Son of God,
R. ora pro nobis.	**R.** pray for us.
Christi defensor sedule,	Diligent protector of Christ,
R. ora pro nobis.	**R.** pray for us.
Almae Familiae praeses,	Head of the Holy Family,
R. ora pro nobis.	**R.** pray for us.
Ioseph iustissime,	Joseph most just,
R. ora pro nobis.	**R.** pray for us.
Ioseph castissime,	Joseph most chaste,
R. ora pro nobis.	**R.** pray for us.
Ioseph prudentissime,	Joseph most prudent,
R. ora pro nobis.	**R.** pray for us.

Ioseph fortissime,	Joseph most strong,
R. ora pro nobis.	**R.** pray for us.
Ioseph oboedientissime,	Joseph, most obedient,
R. ora pro nobis.	**R.** pray for us.
Ioseph fidelissime,	Joseph most faithful,
R. ora pro nobis.	**R.** pray for us.
Speculum patientiae,	Mirror of patience,
R. ora pro nobis.	**R.** pray for us.
Amator paupertatis,	Lover of poverty,
R. ora pro nobis.	**R.** pray for us.
Exemplar opificum,	Model of artisans,
R. ora pro nobis.	**R.** pray for us.
Domesticae vitae decus,	Glory of home life,
R. ora pro nobis.	**R.** pray for us.
Custos virginum,	Guardian of virgins,
R. ora pro nobis.	**R.** pray for us.
Familiarum columen,	Pillar of families,
R. ora pro nobis.	**R.** pray for us.

Solatium miserorum, **R.** ora pro nobis.	Solace of the wretched, **R.** pray for us.
Spes aegrotantium, **R.** ora pro nobis.	Hope of the sick, **R.** pray for us.
Patrone morientium, **R.** ora pro nobis.	Patron of the dying, **R.** pray for us.
Terror daemonum, **R.** ora pro nobis.	Terror of demons, **R.** pray for us.
Protector sanctae Ecclesiae, **R.** ora pro nobis.	Protector of the Holy Church, **R.** pray for us.
Agnus Dei, qui tollis peccata mundi, **R.** parce nobis, Domine.	Lamb of God, who takes away the sins of the world, **R.** spare us, O Lord.
Agnus Dei, qui tollis peccata mundi, **R.** exaudi nobis, Domine.	Lamb of God, who takes away the sins of the world, **R.** graciously hear us, O Lord.
Agnus Dei, qui tollis peccata mundi, **R.** miserere nobis.	Lamb of God, who takes away the sins of the world, **R.** have mercy on us.

V. Constituit eum dominum domus suae.

V. He made him the lord of his household.

R. Et principem omnis possessionis suae.

R. And prince over all his possessions.

Oremus: Deus, qui in ineffabili providentia beatum Ioseph sanctissimae Genetricis tuae Sponsum eligere dignatus es, praesta, quaesumus, ut quem protectorem veneramur in terris, intercessorem habere mereamur in caelis: Qui vivis et regnas in saecula saeculorum. Amen.

Let us pray: O God, in Thy ineffable providence Thou wert pleased to choose Blessed Joseph to be the spouse of Thy most holy Mother, grant, we beg Thee, that we may be worthy to have him for our intercessor in Heaven whom on earth we venerate as our Protector; Thou who livest and reignest forever and ever. Amen.

HOLY CLOAK OF ST. JOSEPH

It is natural and worthy that as Blessed Joseph ministered to all the needs of the family at Nazareth and girt it about with his protection, he should now cover with the cloak of his heavenly patronage, and defend, the Church of Jesus Christ. – Pope Leo XIII, Quamquam Pluries

In the name of the + Father, and of the Son, and of the Holy Spirit. Amen.

Jesus, Mary and Joseph, I give Thee my heart and my soul.

Recite the "Glory Be" three times in thanksgiving to the Most Holy Trinity for having exalted St. Joseph to a position of such exceptional dignity.

Glory be to the Father, and to the Son, and to the Holy Spirit, as it was in the beginning is now, and ever shall be, world without end. Amen.

OFFERING

O Glorious Patriarch St. Joseph, I humbly prostrate myself before Thee. I beg the Lord Jesus, thine Immaculate Spouse, the Blessed Virgin Mary, and all the Angels and Saints in the Heavenly Court, to join me in this devotion. I offer thee this precious cloak, while pledging my sincerest faith and devotion. I promise to do all in my power to honour thee throughout my lifetime to prove my love for thee. Help me, St. Joseph. Assist me now and throughout my lifetime, but especially at the moment of my death, as thou wert assisted by Jesus and Mary, that I may join thee one day in Heaven and there honour thee for all eternity. Amen.

PRAYER I

Hail O Glorious St. Joseph, thou who art entrusted with the priceless treasures of Heaven and Earth and virgin-father of Him Who doth nourish all the creatures of the universe. Thou art, after Mary, the Saint most worthy of our love and devotion. Thou alone, above all the Saints, wert chosen for that supreme honour of rearing, guiding, nourishing and even embracing the Messiah, Whom so many kings and prophets would have so desired to behold. St. Joseph, save my soul and obtain for me from the Divine Mercy of God that petition for which I humbly pray. And for the Holy Souls in Purgatory, grant a great comfort from their pain.

Recite the "Glory Be" three times in thanksgiving to the Most Holy Trinity for having exalted St. Joseph to a position of such exceptional dignity.

Glory be to the Father, and to the Son, and to the Holy Spirit, as it was in the beginning is now, and ever shall be, world without end. Amen.

PRAYER II

O powerful St. Joseph, thou wert proclaimed the Patron of the Universal Church, therefore, I invoke thee, above all the other Saints, as the greatest protector of the afflicted, and I offer countless blessings to thy most generous heart, always ready to help in any need. To thee, O Glorious St. Joseph, come the widows, the orphans, the abandoned, the afflicted, and the oppressed. There is no sorrow, heartache or anguish which thou hast not consoled. Deign, I beseech thee, to use on my behalf those gifts which God hast given thee, until I too shall be granted the answer to my petition. And thou, Holy Souls in Purgatory, pray to St. Joseph for me.

254

Recite the "Glory Be" three times in thanksgiving to the Most Holy Trinity for having exalted St. Joseph to a position of such exceptional dignity.

Glory be to the Father, and to the Son, and to the Holy Spirit, as it was in the beginning is now, and ever shall be, world without end. Amen.

PRAYER III

Countless are those who have prayed to thee before me and have received comfort and peace, graces and favours. My heart, so sad and sorrowful, cannot find rest in the midst of this trial which besets me. O Glorious St. Joseph, thou knowest all my needs even before I set them forth in prayer. Thou knowest how important this petition is for me. I prostrate myself before thee as I sigh under the heavy weight of the problem which confronts me. There is no human heart in which I can confide my sorrow; and even if I should find a compassionate creature who would be willing to assist me, still he would be unable to help me. Only thou can help me in my sorrow, St. Joseph, and I beg thee to hear my plea. O St. Joseph, comforter of the afflicted, have pity on my sorrow and pity on those Poor Souls who place so much hope in their prayers to thee.

Recite the "Glory Be" three times in thanksgiving to the Most Holy Trinity for having exalted St. Joseph to a position of such exceptional dignity.

Glory be to the Father, and to the Son, and to the Holy Spirit, as it was in the beginning is now, and ever shall be, world without end. Amen.

PRAYER IV

O Sublime Patriarch St. Joseph, because of thy perfect obedience to God, thou mayest intercede for me. For thy holy life full of grace and merit, hear my prayer. For thy most sweet name, help me. For your most holy tears, comfort me. For thy seven sorrows, intercede for me. For your seven joys, console me. From all harm of body and soul, deliver me. From all danger and disaster, save me. Assist me with thy intercession and seek for me, all that is necessary for my salvation and particularly the favour of which I now stand in such great need.

Recite the "Glory Be" three times in thanksgiving to the Most Holy Trinity for having exalted St. Joseph to a position of such exceptional dignity.

Glory be to the Father, and to the Son, and to the Holy Spirit, as it was in the beginning is now, and ever shall be, world without end. Amen.

PRAYER V

O Glorious St. Joseph, countless are the graces and favours which thou hast obtained for afflicted souls. Illness of every nature, those who are oppressed, persecuted, betrayed, bereft of all human comfort, even those in need of their life bread - all who imploreth thy powerful intercession are comforted in their affliction. Do not permit, O dearest St. Joseph, that I alone be the only one of all who hast appealed to thee, to be denied this petition which I so earnestly beg of thee. Show thy kindness and generosity even to me, that I may cry out in thanksgiving, "Eternal glory to our Holy Patriarch St. Joseph, my great protector on Earth and the defender of the Holy Souls in Purgatory."

Recite the "Glory Be" three times in thanksgiving to the Most Holy Trinity for having exalted St. Joseph to a position of such exceptional dignity.

Glory be to the Father, and to the Son, and to the Holy Spirit, as it was in the beginning is now, and ever shall be, world without end. Amen.

PRAYER VI

Eternal Father, Who art in Heaven, through the merits of Jesus and Mary, I beg Thee to grant my petition. In the name of Jesus and Mary I prostrate myself before Thy Divine presence and I beseech Thee to accept my hopeful plea to persevere in my prayers that I may be numbered among the throngs of those who live under the patronage of St. Joseph. Extend Thy blessing on this precious treasury of prayers which I today offer to him as a pledge of my devotion.

Recite the "Glory Be" three times in thanksgiving to the Most Holy Trinity for having exalted St. Joseph to a position of such exceptional dignity.

Glory be to the Father, and to the Son, and to the Holy Spirit, as it was in the beginning is now, and ever shall be, world without end. Amen.

PRAYER VII

Glorious St Joseph, spouse of the Blessed Virgin Mary and virginal father of Jesus, look upon me and watch over me; lead me on the path of sanctifying grace; take heed of the urgent needs which I now beg you to envelop within the folds of your fatherly cloak. Dismiss those obstacles and difficulties standing in the way of my prayer and grant that the happy answer to my petition may serve for the greater glory of God and my eternal salvation. As a pledge of my undying gratitude, I promise to spread the word of your glory while offering thanks to the Lord for having so blessed your power and might in Heaven and Earth.

Recite the "Glory Be" three times in thanksgiving to the Most Holy Trinity for having exalted St. Joseph to a position of such exceptional dignity.

Glory be to the Father, and to the Son, and to the Holy Spirit, as it was in the beginning is now, and ever shall be, world without end. Amen.

SUPPLICATIONS

St. Joseph, pray that Jesus may come into my soul and sanctify me.

St. Joseph, pray that Jesus may come into my heart and inspire it with charity.

St. Joseph, pray that Jesus may come into my mind and enlighten it.

St. Joseph, pray that Jesus may guide my will and strengthen it.

St. Joseph, pray that Jesus may direct my thoughts and purify them.

St. Joseph, pray that Jesus may guide my desires and direct them.

St. Joseph, pray that Jesus may look upon my deeds and extend His blessings.

St. Joseph, pray that Jesus may inflame me with love for Him.

St. Joseph, request for me from Jesus the imitation of thy virtues.

MEMORARE

Remember O most chaste spouse of the Blessed Virgin Mary, my good protector St Joseph, that never was it known that anyone who came to your protection, and sought your intercession was left unaided. Confidently I prostrate myself before you and fervently beg for your powerful intervention. O Virgin-Father of our dear Redeemer, despise not my petition, but in your mercy, hear and answer me. Amen.

LITANY OF ST. JOSEPH (see page 247)

CLOSING PRAYERS OF THE HOLY CLOAK

Recite the "Glory Be" three times in thanksgiving to the Most Holy Trinity for having exalted St. Joseph to a position of such exceptional dignity.

Glory be to the Father, and to the Son, and to the Holy Spirit, as it was in the beginning is now, and ever shall be, world without end. Amen.

O Glorious Patriarch St. Joseph, thou who wert chosen by God above all men to be the earthly head of the most holy of families, I beseech thee to accept me within the folds of thy holy cloak, that thou mayest become the guardian and custodian of my soul.

O Wondrous St. Joseph, from this moment on, I choose thee as my father, my protector, my counselor, my patron and I beseech thee to place in thy custody my body, my soul, all that I am, all that I possess, my life and my death.

O Loving St. Joseph, look upon me as one of thy children; defend me from the treachery of my enemies, invisible or otherwise, assist me at all times in all my necessities; console me in the bitterness of my life, and especially at the hour of my death. Say but one word for me to the Divine Redeemer Whom thou wert deemed worthy to hold in thine arms, and to the Blessed Virgin Mary, thy most chaste spouse. Request for me those blessings which will lead me to salvation. Include me amongst those who art most dear to thee and I shall set forth to prove myself worthy of thy special patronage. + Amen.

THE CHAPLET OF ST. JOSEPH
Using Rosary Beads

1. Crucifix or Medal - Sign of the Cross & Apostles' Creed: In the name of the Father, and of the Son, and of the Holy Spirit. Amen.

I believe in God, the Father Almighty, Creator of Heaven and earth; and in Jesus Christ, His only Son our Lord, Who was conceived by the Holy Spirit, born of the Virgin Mary, suffered under Pontius Pilate, was crucified, died, and was buried. He descended into Hell; on the third day He rose again from the dead; He ascended into Heaven, and is seated at the right hand of God, the Father almighty; from thence He shall come to judge the living and the dead. I believe in the Holy Spirit, the holy Catholic Church, the communion of saints, the forgiveness of sins, the resurrection of the body and life everlasting. Amen.

2. Our Father: Our Father, Who art in Heaven, hallowed be Thy name; Thy kingdom come; Thy will be done on earth as it is in Heaven. Give us this day our daily bread; and forgive us our trespasses as we forgive those who trespass against us; and lead us not into temptation but deliver us from evil. Amen.

3. St. Pius X Prayer: O Joseph, virgin father of Jesus, pure spouse of the Virgin Mary, pray for us daily to the Son of God, that, armed with the weapons of His grace, we may fight as we ought in life, and be crowned by Him in death. Amen.

4. Hail Mary: Hail Mary, full of grace, the Lord is with thee. Blessed art thou among women, and blessed is the fruit of thy womb, Jesus. Holy Mary, Mother of God, pray for us sinners, now and at the hour of our death. Amen.

5. Glory Be: Glory be to the Father, and to the Son, and to the Holy Spirit. As it was in the beginning, is now, and ever shall be, world without end. Amen.

6. Mystery & Our Father: Announce and read the reflection for the mystery, then pray the **Our Father.**

7. Hail Joseph x 10: Hail Joseph, Son of David, God is with you! Blessed are you among men and blessed is our Lord Jesus Christ! Holy Joseph, Guardian of the Redeemer, pray for us and be with us, now and as we sigh our last breath. Amen.

8. Holy Family Aspiration: Jesus, Mary, and Joseph, I give you my heart and my soul. Jesus, Mary, and Joseph, assist me in my last agony. Jesus, Mary, and Joseph, may I breathe forth my soul in peace with you.

After praying the five mysteries:

9. Ancient Prayer to St. Joseph (see page 243)

10. The Divine Praises & Sign of the Cross: Blessed be God. Blessed be His Holy Name. Blessed be Jesus Christ, true God and true Man. Blessed be the Name of Jesus. Blessed be His Most Sacred Heart. Blessed be His Most Precious Blood. Blessed be Jesus in the Most Holy Sacrament of the Altar. Blessed be the Holy Spirit, the Paraclete. Blessed be the great Mother of God, Mary most Holy. Blessed be her Holy and Immaculate Conception. Blessed be her Glorious Assumption. Blessed be the name of Mary, Virgin and Mother. Blessed be St. Joseph, her most chaste spouse. Blessed be God in His Angels and in His Saints.

In the name of the + Father, and of the Son, and of the Holy Spirit. Amen.

JOYFUL MYSTERIES OF ST. JOSEPH

1. Sanctification of Joseph: St. Joseph had three graces which were special to him. Firstly, he was sanctified in his mother's womb. Secondly, he was confirmed in grace. Thirdly, that he was always exempt from impurity. – St. Alphonsus de Liguori

2. Holy Espousals: God spoke to the heart of the high priest, inspiring him to give each of the young men a dry stick; by a sign He would show whom He had chosen to be the spouse of Mary. While they prayed, the rod which Joseph held was seen to blossom and a dove of purest white descended upon him. And so, the priest espoused Mary to the most chaste and holy of men, St. Joseph. – Venerable Maria de Agreda

3. Annunciation to Joseph: The angel of the Lord appeared to him in a dream, saying, "Joseph, son of David ... the child conceived in Mary is of the Holy Spirit; she will give birth to a son, and you will call him Jesus: He will save His people from their sins." – St. Matthew 1:20-21

4. Birth of Jesus: On that holy night, in Bethlehem, with Mary and the Child, is Joseph, to whom the Heavenly Father entrusted the daily care of His Son, which Joseph carried out in humility. Think of the love of Joseph who was the first man to set eyes on the human face of God. – Pope Benedict XVI

5. Life with Jesus and Mary: What flames of holy love must have been burning in the heart of Joseph, who for thirty years conversed with Jesus Christ, and listened to His words of eternal life! – St. Alphonsus de Liguori

SORROWFUL MYSTERIES OF ST. JOSEPH

1. Joseph Resolves to Leave Mary: Joseph, being a just man, and not willing to make her a public example, was minded to put Mary away privately. – St. Matthew 1:19

2. Poverty of Jesus' Birth: Joseph is a witness to the birth of the Son of God, which took place in conditions that, humanly speaking, were embarrassing – a first announcement of that self-emptying which Christ freely accepted. – St. John Paul II

3. Simeon's Prophecy: This child is destined for the falling and the rising of many in Israel, and to be a sign that will be opposed. And a sword shall pierce through Mary's soul, that the thoughts of many hearts may be revealed. – St. Luke 2:34-35

4. Exile in Egypt: Joseph guarded from death the Child threatened by a monarch's jealousy, and found for Him a refuge; in the miseries of the journey and in the bitterness of exile he was always the companion, the assistance, and the upholder of the Virgin and of Jesus. – Pope Leo XIII

5. Loss of the Adolescent Jesus: When He was twelve years old, Jesus' parents brought Him to Jerusalem to celebrate the Passover. On their return, the boy Jesus stayed behind in Jerusalem, but His parents did not know it. Assuming that He was in the group of travelers, they went a day's journey. Then they started to look for Him among their relatives and friends. When they did not find Him, they returned to Jerusalem to search for Him. After three days they found Him in the Temple, sitting among the teachers, listening to them and asking them questions. ... and His mother said to Him, "Son, why have you done this to us? Behold, your father and I have searched for you in sorrow." – St. Luke 2:41-48

GLORIOUS MYSTERIES OF ST. JOSEPH

1. Holy Death of Joseph: After having faithfully served Jesus and Mary, St. Joseph reached the end of his life in the house at Nazareth. There, surrounded by angels, assisted by Jesus Christ the King of angels, and by Mary, his spouse, filled with the peace of paradise, he departed from this life. – St. Alphonsus de Liguori

2. Glorification of Joseph in Heaven: How could we doubt that our Lord raised glorious St. Joseph up into Heaven, body and soul? For Joseph had the honour and grace of carrying Jesus so often in his blessed arms. St. Joseph is therefore in Heaven body and soul, without a doubt. – St. Francis de Sales

3. Intercession of St. Joseph: St. Joseph, with the love and generosity with which he guarded Jesus, so too will he guard your soul, and as he defended Him from Herod, so will he defend your soul from the devil! All the care that the Patriarch St. Joseph has for Jesus, he has for you and will always help you with his patronage. He will not allow your heart to be estranged from Jesus. Go to Joseph with extreme confidence, because I do not remember having asked anything from St. Joseph, without having obtained it readily. – St. Padre Pio

4. Patron of Workers: The glorious Patriarch St. Joseph, humble and just worker of Nazareth, has given to all Christians an example of a perfect life through diligent labour and admirable union with Jesus and Mary. – Venerable Pope Pius XII

5. Patron of the Church: In these latter times in which a monstrous and most abominable war has been declared against the Church of Christ ... we should more efficaciously implore the ... intercession of St. Joseph. Hence, by a special decree We solemnly declare the blessed patriarch Joseph to be Patron of the Universal Church! – Blessed Pope Pius IX

ST. JOSEPH IN SCRIPTURE

GOSPEL OF ST. MATTHEW
Douay-Rheims Version
1:16, 18-25, 2:13-15, 19-23, 13:55

[16] And Jacob begot **Joseph** the husband of Mary, of whom was born Jesus, who is called Christ. [18] Now the generation of Christ was in this wise. When as His mother Mary was espoused to **Joseph**, before they came together, she was found with child, of the Holy Ghost.

[19] Whereupon **Joseph** her husband, being a just man, and not willing publicly to expose her, was minded to put her away privately.

[20] But while he thought on these things, behold the angel of the Lord appeared to him in his sleep, saying: **Joseph**, son of David, fear not to take unto thee Mary thy wife, for that which is conceived in her, is of the Holy Ghost.

[21] And she shall bring forth a son: and thou shalt call his name Jesus … [24] And **Joseph** rising up from sleep, did as the angel of the Lord had commanded him, and took unto him his wife. [25] And he knew her not, and she brought forth her firstborn son: and he called his name Jesus.

2:13 And after they were departed, behold an angel of the Lord appeared in sleep to **Joseph**, saying: Arise, and take the child and his mother, and fly into Egypt: and be there until I shall tell thee. For it will come to pass that Herod will seek the child to destroy him.

[14] **Who** arose, and took the child and his mother by night, and retired into Egypt: and he was there until the death of Herod:

¹⁵ That it might be fulfilled which the Lord spoke by the prophet, saying: Out of Egypt have I called my son. ... ¹⁹ But when Herod was dead, behold an angel of the Lord appeared in sleep to **Joseph** in Egypt, ²⁰ saying: Arise, and take the child and his mother, and go into the land of Israel. For they are dead that sought the life of the child. ²¹ Who arose, and took the child and his mother, and came into the land of Israel.

²² But hearing that Archelaus reigned in Judea in the room of Herod his father, Joseph was afraid to go thither: and being warned in sleep retired into the quarters of Galilee. ²³ And coming he dwelt in a city called Nazareth: that it might be fulfilled which was said by prophets: That he shall be called a Nazarene.

13:55 Is not this the **carpenter's** son? Is not his mother called Mary...?

GOSPEL OF ST. LUKE
1:26-27, 2:4-5, 16, 22, 27, 33, 39, 41-51, 3:23

1:26 And in the sixth month, the angel Gabriel was sent from God into a city of Galilee, called Nazareth, ²⁷ to a virgin espoused to a man whose name was **Joseph**, of the house of David; and the virgin's name was Mary.

2:4 And **Joseph** also went up from Galilee, out of the city of Nazareth into Judea, to the city of David, which is called Bethlehem: because he was of the house and family of David, ⁵ to be enrolled with Mary his espoused wife, who was with child.

¹⁶ And the shepherds came with haste; and they found Mary and **Joseph**, and the infant lying in the manger.

²² And after the days of her purification, according to the Law of Moses, were accomplished, Mary and **Joseph** carried him to Jerusalem, to present him to the Lord.

²⁷ And his **parents** brought in the child Jesus, to do for him according to the custom of the law ...

³³ And his **father** and mother were wondering at those things which were spoken concerning him.

³⁹ And after **they** had performed all things according to the law of the Lord, they returned into Galilee, to their city Nazareth.

⁴¹ And his **parents** went every year to Jerusalem, at the solemn day of the Pasch, ⁴² And when he was twelve years old, they going up into Jerusalem, according to the custom of the feast,

⁴³ And having fulfilled the days, when **they** returned, the child Jesus remained in Jerusalem; and his parents knew it not.

⁴⁴ And thinking that he was in the company, **they** came a day's journey, and sought him among their kinsfolks and acquaintance. ⁴⁵ And not finding him, they returned into Jerusalem, seeking him.

⁴⁶ And it came to pass, that, after three days, **they** found him in the Temple, sitting in the midst of the doctors, hearing them, and asking them questions. ⁴⁷ And all that heard him were astonished at his wisdom and his answers. ⁴⁸ And seeing him, they wondered.

And his mother said to him: Son, why hast thou done so to us? Behold thy **father** and I have sought thee sorrowing.

⁴⁹ And he said to them: How is it that you sought me? Did you not know that I must be about my father's business? ⁵⁰ And **they** understood not the word that he spoke unto them. ⁵¹ And he went down with them, and came to Nazareth, and was subject to them. And his mother kept all these words in her heart.

3:23 And Jesus himself was beginning about the age of thirty years; being (as it was supposed) the son of **Joseph**, who was of Heli ...

GOSPEL OF ST. JOHN
1:45, 6:42

1:45 We have found him of whom Moses in the law, and the prophets did write, Jesus the son of **Joseph of Nazareth**.

6:42 they said: Is not this Jesus, the son of **Joseph**, whose father and mother we know? How then saith he, I came down from Heaven?

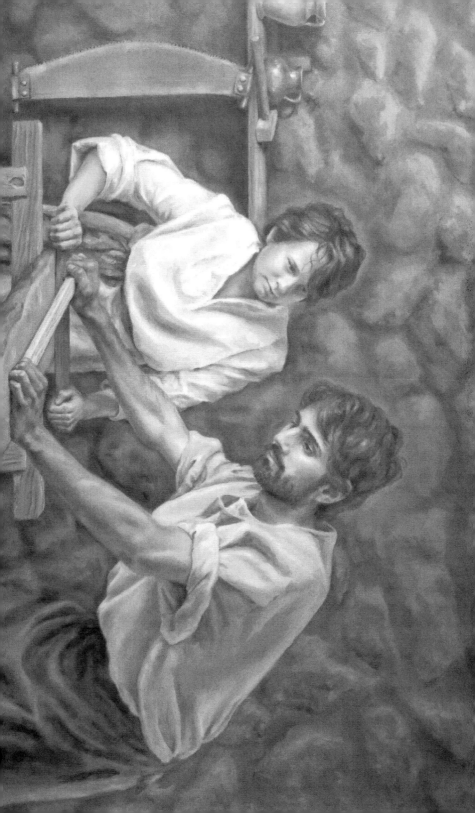

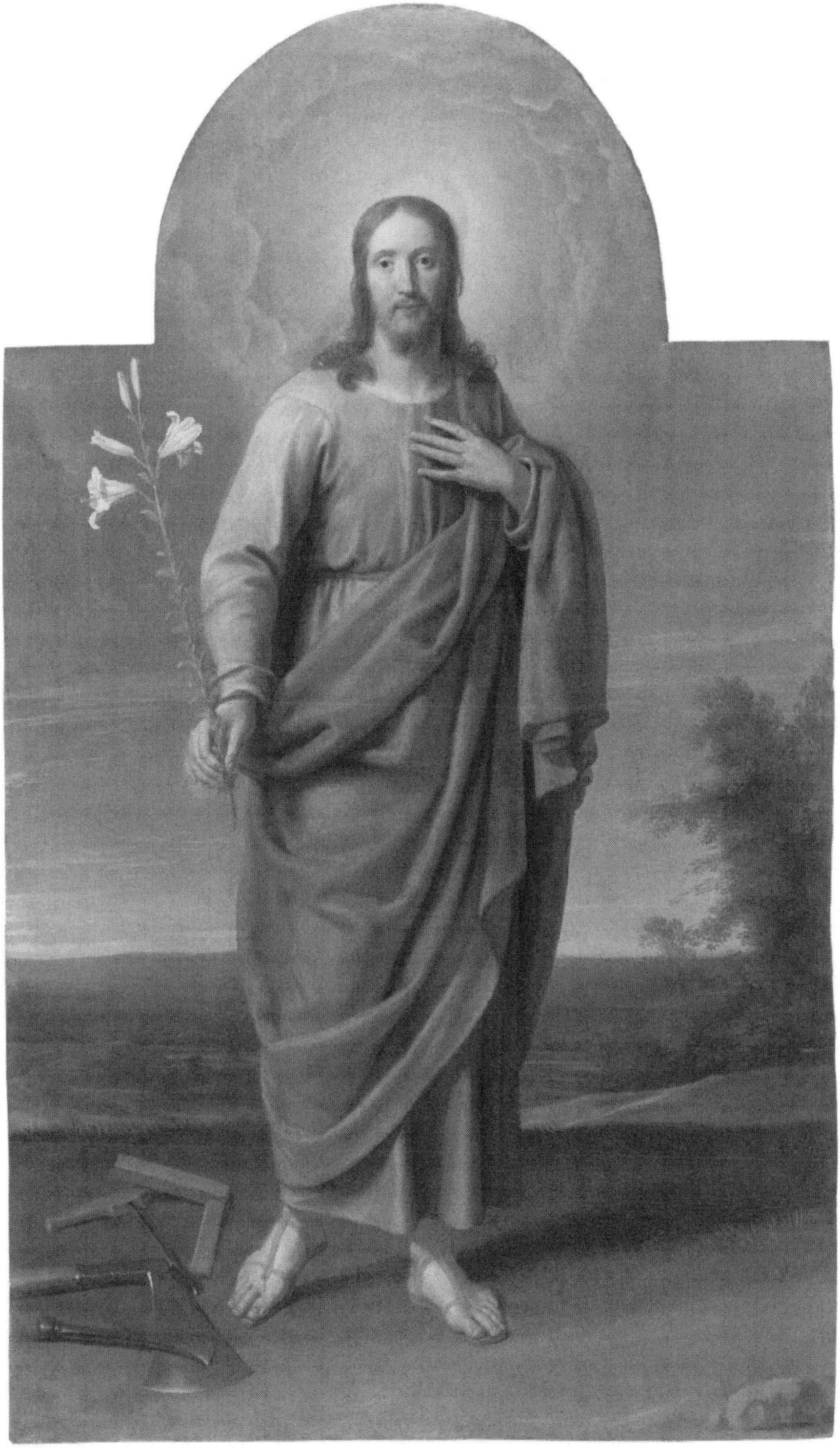

Videbam... quasi Solem, Luna, & Stellas adorare me.

BIBLIOGRAPHY

THE HOLY BIBLE (see page 2 for translations used)

THE HOLY SEE
www.vatican.va

THE LIFE OF ST. JOSEPH
Baij, Mo. Cecilia

THE MYSTICAL CITY OF GOD
De Agreda, Ven. Maria

THE LIFE OF THE BLESSED VIRGIN MARY
Emmerich, Bl. Anne Catherine

THE LIFE OF JESUS CHRIST
Emmerich, Bl. Anne Catherine

THE LIFE AND GLORIES OF ST. JOSEPH
Thompson, Edward Healy

REDEMPTORIS CUSTOS
Pope St. John Paul II. Libreria Editrice Vaticana, 1989

LE VOCI CHE DA TUTTI
Pope St. John XXIII. Libreria Editrice Vaticana, 1961

DIVINI REDEMPTORIS
Pope Pius XI. Libreria Editrice Vaticana, 1937

BONUM SANE
Pope Benedict XV. Libreria Editrice Vaticana, 1920

QUAMQUAM PLURIES
Pope Leo XIII. Libreria Editrice Vaticana, 1889

INCLYTUM PATRIARCHAM
Bl. Pope Pius IX. Libreria Editrice Vaticana, 1871

ART CREDITS

St. Joseph Holding the Child Jesus – page 63
Esteban Murillo, 17th Century

Young St. Joseph Offers His Virginity to God – page 289

Marriage of Mary and Joseph – page 271
Luca Giordano, 1688

The Dream of St. Joseph – page 272
Philippe de Champaigne, 1643

The Flight into Egypt – page 273
Bartolome Murillo, 1648

The Holy Family with Sts. Elisabeth and John – page 274
Simon Vouet, 17th Century

St. Joseph Holding the Child Jesus – page 275
Margherita Gallucci, 2015

Heaven and Earth Trinities with Sts. Augustine and Catherine – page 276

Holy Family in the Carpenter Shop – page 277
Aristides Artal, 2000

Finding Jesus in the Temple – page 278
Philippe de Champaigne, 17TH Century

Paternitas – page 279
Kate Capato, 2017 – www.VisualGrace.org

St. Joseph and The Boy Jesus – page 280
Nacho Valdes, 2016 – www.NachoValdes.com

St. Joseph – page 281
Philippe de Champaigne, 1650

St. Joseph – page 282
Ernst Deger, 19th Century

The Lily and the Carpenter – page 283
Gwyneth Thompson-Briggs – www.GwynethThompsonBriggs.com

Holy Trinity and Holy Family – page 284
Carlo Dolci, 1630

Death of St. Joseph – page 285
Padre Fedele Tirrito, 1760

Assumption of St. Joseph – page 286
French School, 17th Century

Coronation of St. Joseph – page 287
Juan de Valdes Leal, 1670

St. Joseph Patron of the Church – page 288
Giuseppe Rollini, 1893

St. Joseph Viceroy of Christ – page 289
17th century

St. Joseph with Child Jesus – page 290
Cusco School, 17th Century

St. Joseph with Child Jesus – page 291
Yuriy Kuku, 2017 – www.facebook.com/ArteYuriy.Kuku

St. Joseph and the Child Jesus – page 292
Dominic Chetcuti, 2019

Home – page 293
Kate Capato, 2017 – www.VisualGrace.org

Coronation of St. Joseph by Jesus and Mary – page 294
José de Ibarra, 1735

The Chaste Heart of St. Joseph – page 295
Giovanni Gasparro, 2013 – www.GiovanniGasparro.com

Death of St. Joseph – page 296
Giovanni Gasparro – www.GiovanniGasparro.com

Assumption of St. Joseph – page 297
Giovanni Battista Gaulli

St. Joseph Terror of Demons – page 298
Dominic Chetcuti, 2018

Modern St. Joseph – page 299
Gracie Morbitzer, 2016 – www.TheModernSaints.com